TALES OF AN IRISH REBEL

THE LIFE STORY OF
RICHARD EMMETT DILLON

Above, left: Dick Dillon at about two years.

Above, right: Dick Dillon's Sixth Form Canterbury Photo. 1952.

Left: Dick Dillon in mid-career.

TALES OF AN IRISH REBEL

THE LIFE STORY OF RICHARD EMMETT DILLON

Written by

LOU MANDLER

Based on interviews with

DICK AND PHYLLIS DILLON

2017

www.bookstandpublishing.com

Published by
Bookstand Publishing
Morgan Hill, CA 95037
4542_3

ISBN 978-1-63498-546-8

Printed in the United States of America

DEDICATION

TO PHYLLIS, MY WIFE OF SIXTY-TWO YEARS,

SIX WONDERFUL CHILDREN,

EIGHT GRANDCHILDREN,

AND ONE GREAT GRANDSON

FOREWORD

For some time my wife, Phyllis, has been asking me, bugging me, pleading that I write my memoirs. She has loved many of the stories accumulated over our years together—sixty-five years of friendship and sixty-two of marriage. By the fall of 2016, the time had come, triggered by a major medical problem after which the doctors at Mayo Clinic told me I had two years to continue to enjoy my wife, family, friends, and nightly martinis.

I have had great respect for Lou Mandler from the many years of my association with Canterbury. I decided she would be the one to write it. Much to my surprise, she agreed when I suggested the project to her.

Thanks, Phyllis and family, for a wonderful ride, and thanks, Lou.

Richard E. Dillon. April 2017

PROLOGUE

On a brilliant fall afternoon in Jackson, Wyoming, my husband JP and I walked with Phyllis and Dick Dillon towards the outdoor setting of the wedding of Patrick Sheehy, son of our mutual friends, Tom and Betsy Sheehy. The Snake River, fringed with aspens flaunting their autumnal yellow, lay before us as we chatted a bit. Then Dick asked me in his characteristic blunt way, "Will you write my life story?" Without hesitation I said, "Sure."

Until then, I had known Dick as a graduate and trustee of Canterbury School, where JP and I had worked for decades, and as a grandparent and de facto parent of his and Phyllis's grandsons, Derrick and Brian Dillon. As a trustee and parent, Dick did not blend into the background, and it wasn't his shock of white hair or his substantial 5'8"physical stature that made him stand out. Dick talked to everyone and anyone, and when Dick talked to you, his remarkable, crystal blue eyes gave you his full attention. Then there was the straight forward talk. Dick never beat around the bush; if he wanted to know something, he asked without pussyfooting. He was just as direct with his observations and opinions.

In the years that Dick was associated with Canterbury, I had learned something of his life—that he had owned a successful Hispanic advertising agency, and when he gave Canterbury's memorable graduation speech in 2014, he built his message around failure he had experienced during his time in the military in the 1950s.

In November of 2016, armed with recorder and computer, I spent four days at Dick and Phyllis's Vero Beach home to begin to gather information for Dick's life story.

Dick and I sat every morning at the breakfast table with the patio, pool, and canal in sight. Dick, a hundred pounds lighter than at his prime fighting weight, showed the effects of the last year's illness, but he still wore his trademark pink polo shirt, and his memory for names and quotes was spot on, his sense of humor very much intact, and those crystal blue eyes were still expressive. Dick told his stories into the recorder, stopping occasionally to tell me how to spell a name or respond to my clarifying questions. In the afternoons, I transcribed his stories, which Dick checked for accuracy. Phyllis's memories, told not at the breakfast table but from the patio table, added a rich dimension to this narrative. Later, Dick and Phyllis's daughter Patty Allman shared some memories, adding still another layer.

After I returned to Connecticut to write, Dick and I corresponded through email. The Dillon project was a researcher's delight because many of the people Dick and Phyllis knew were national figures on whom I found interesting background information to add to the narrative. In March of 2017, I returned to Vero with a draft, and we recorded more stories and filled in gaps. Back in Connecticut, Canterbury's Marc Vanasse worked his magic on scanning, formatting, and captioning photos. The women in my writers group--Anne Batterson, Chivas Sandage, Sally Terrell, and Sherry Horton--made some valuable suggestions. Sherry Horton and JP Mandler each gave the manuscript a careful read.

My collaboration with Dick and Phyllis brought out much more than a simple chronicle of Dick's successful career path. Dick's story isn't a recital of "I did this, and then I did this," although that was the framework of his narrative. More fascinating is the character that drove this life story and the rich life it created.

Early in his career, Dick formed an admiration for Winston Churchill. This admiration is understandable given how Dick's life illustrates such Churchill quotes as "Never give in - never, never, never, never, in nothing great or small, large or petty, never give in except to convictions of honour and good sense."

Dick commented early in our interviews, "I was always a rebel." Call it being a rebel, call it stubbornness, or call it determination, this stout belief in his own ideas and standards never left him. He stuck by what he knew to be right even if he knew it would get him fired. And it did get him fired. More than once. But as Phyllis, who is remarkable in her own right, said, "I have always had such incredible confidence in him. I was never shaken to the core. I was empathetic, but always knew he would be OK."

Dick Dillon's story is that of an Irish Catholic boy from Brooklyn who became a sure-minded, successful corporate leader. This book follows Dick's journey on to Canterbury School, Princeton University, the U.S. Army and jobs in New York, Mexico, Europe, Canada, Colorado, and California.

Very early in this journey, Dick found an outgoing, energetic, "rock" of a life partner—Phyllis Freschi from St. Louis. And, along the way, they became parents of six: Richard, Jr., Patty, Michael, Stephen, Scott, and Bill.

To be complete, Dick Dillon's story must not only be about his successful career, but also about the kind of guy he is—what formed him, what motivates him, what his passions are, what his essential qualities are. How can you say you know Dick Dillon unless you know his love of baseball, his passion for golf, that he can belt out a rousing "Danny Boy," that he has an amazing array of friends, that one of his proudest roles is as patriarch of the Dillon clan? Read on.

Lou Mandler. April 2017

TABLE OF CONTENTS

CHAPTER ONE

THE BEGINNING TO 1947

Dick Dillon says he is "very much of Irish extraction," but there are no stories about Dillon forebears arriving in America during the famine or of any relatives left behind in Ireland. The family has not been able to ascertain when the first Dillons or, on his mother's side, the first O'Haras, arrived from Ireland. At one point, Dick asked his great aunt Mary Dillon, who was born in America in 1885, "Mary, tell me about our family. When did they come over from Ireland?" She responded. "I don't know. I'll tell you anything you want to know about New York City in the 1900s, but nothing about Ireland."

Mary Dillon is early evidence that the family genes create people with brains, ambition and a willingness to work. Mary E. Dillon, who never graduated from high school, became the "office boy" (as she called it) and the only female employee at Brooklyn Borough Gas Company in 1902, at the age of 17. At 20, she became office manager; in 1924, she was named general manager and vice president, and in 1926, at the age of 41, she was named CEO, the first woman in the world to head a utility company. Although she married, she kept her birth name. In a radio address in 1935, Eleanor Roosevelt included Mary Dillon as one of "eleven women whose achievements make it safe to say the world is progressing." Included among the other eleven were Secretary of State Frances Perkins, social worker Jane Addams, and Amelia Earhart. Mary Dillon went on to become President of the New York City Board of Education under Mayor Fiorello LaGuardia, and she was active in cultural affairs. In June and July, 2014, the digital publication *Brownstoner* published a four-part story, "Miss Dillon's Gas Company." The 1998 *Understanding The Great Gatsby* (Greenwood Press) discusses Mary Dillon and reprints an article about her from a 1929 *American Magazine.* Both publications underscore how unique Mary Dillon's accomplishments were for a woman in the early 1900s.

In the next generation, Dick's father, John Charles Dillon, Jr., was born in New York's Hell's Kitchen in 1895 into an "itinerant Irish family" headed by an alcoholic father. John Dillon dropped out of school in the fifth grade and told his children that in 1905, he went to Coney Island and found work as the midget who was blown out of the cannon in the Trip to the Moon event. Later, he participated in Coney Island's re-enactment of the Battle of the Monitor and Merrimack, the first battle of ironclad warships in the Civil War. His role was to position himself under the stage and maneuver the ship he was assigned to.

Like his aunt Mary, John Dillon, Jr. was another Dillon who didn't let lack of education stymie his progress. He began working for Wander Press in his twenties and established his own printing company, J.C. Dillon Company, in 1934. He had two sisters and a brother, Philip, who became a Monsignor. By the time John Dillon founded the J.C. Dillon Company, he had married Irene O'Hara and they had four children—John III (Jack) born in 1920; Robert born in 1922, who died in 1927 from a burst appendix; Irene (Renee) born in 1927; and Richard (Dick) born in 1933.

Despite the absence of information about family origins in Ireland, the Dillon Irish lineage was a point of pride. John Dillon belonged to the Sons of St. Patrick, and the family parish in Brooklyn, Holy Innocents, was predominantly Irish. Dick's classmates in the Holy Innocents school had names like Kelly and O'Connor. John and Irene Dillon named their second son Robert Emmett after the Irish rebel who was executed in 1803. When Richard Dillon was born six years after his brother died, they also gave him the Emmett middle name. Dick and Phyllis's eldest child, Richard Emmett Dillon, Jr., and their grandson, Derrick Emmett Dillon, keep alive the sense of Irish history and family.

At the time of Dick's birth in Brooklyn's Kings County Hospital, the family was living in a brownstone on Midwood Street and Bedford Avenue, three blocks from Ebbets Field. Young Dick shared a room with his brother Jack and "Uncle Chubby" (Charlie), Irene Dillon's brother. Besides Uncle Chubby, Irene's sisters, Nellie and "Hank" (Regina), lived with the family. Both Nellie and Hank were employed, Nellie as a telephone operator.

Dick's early experiences in Brooklyn helped shape a lifelong passion. "I remember vividly being in the car with Uncle Chubby, looking at a great big wall, and I said, 'Uncle Chubby, what's that?' 'That's Ebbets Field,' he said. He took me to a couple games and I became an avid baseball fan, probably in 1940. Even today I could tell you the entire Dodger Team in 1941. My favorite number was 4, worn by Dolph Camilli who was the MVP first baseman for the Dodgers that year. I ate, drank, and slept baseball."

Dick commented that his uncle Chubby, who took Dick to his first baseball games, was an alcoholic. Dick had already revealed that his grandfather was an alcoholic, and as we proceeded with his life story, more than once, Dick made the point that certain individuals were alcoholics. "The Irish were hard-drinking people," he said. "My father drank too much, my brother drank too much, and my sister drank too much. I probably drank too much, but I was fortunate that it never dominated me. There were times when I was really down, and it was tempting to have a drink and forget about it, but I was able to reject that impulse. You just know instinctively that it's not right."

By the time Dick was five or six, John Dillon's company was doing well enough that the family moved from Midwood Street to a bigger house on Ocean Avenue, known now as the Ditmas area. His success also enabled the family to buy a house in a beach community in Long Branch, New Jersey. As a four or five-year old, Dick would go to the beach during summer mornings and come home at 7:00 at night. "I was a pest on the beach. My brother and his friends one day held me down and wrote 'Bummy Rubenstein' on my back and paraded me up and down the beach so everyone could see it. They created this story that I had been in a basket that floated ashore, and the only one who would take me in was Irene Dillon. And after that, all those people in Long Branch called me Bummy. There are only one or two left, and they still call me that."

During summers at Long Branch, Dick's love of baseball reached a new level. At age ten or eleven, he became part of a softball team that played other teams in the area. The ages of the players on the team ranged from sixteen to the lower twenties, "and here was little Dickie Dillon playing second base. I loved it, and I was pretty good."

At about the same age, Dick's entrepreneurial streak emerged when he was given a box camera. He began taking pictures of family and friends and developing them in the basement of their Brooklyn house. His father made a business card for him with the line, "We develop while you sleep."

"I made some money at that," Dick said. The Dillons still own family photos Dick took at the time.

Among Dick's Brooklyn memories are of the family's Sunday routine. First they went to church, where Dick served as an altar boy and which operated Holy Innocents, his elementary school. Dick remembers going to Mass and Communion every single day during one two-year period. After church on Sundays, the family gathered on the porch, where the adults had whiskey sours. Then came dinner followed by a nap. Towards evening, Dick would walk with his father to the local deli, where John Dillon took pleasure in buying meats, cheeses and other delicacies for the evening repast. Dick associates his father's delight in these purchases with the fact that he, a poor Irish kid from Hell's Kitchen, could afford to buy what he wanted for his family.

During the ten years after Dick was born, his father made the J.C. Dillon Company into a successful business. The family had help, two cars in the garage, and a summer house. Dick began to emulate his father very early. He said, "I had great respect for my father. He was a very, very hard-working man. His company was on 45th Street between Second and Third, and he would come to work in his derby and Chesterfield. He was always quick to say 'Hello,' knew the names of all the workers and was quick to tip them for any kind of service. He was known as the Mayor of 45th Street by the people who worked in that area, the guys who ran the elevators and things. He was beloved."

The J.C. Dillon printing company prospered even during the Depression and World War II. Bethlehem Steel, a client, was still doing well during the Depression, and during the War, Bethlehem Steel did very well. Other clients were Nestle, Revere Copper and Brass, and Philip Morris.

Dick admits that his admiration for his father and the achievements of others in the family fueled his own ambition. His sister Renee was president of her class at Sacred Heart of Noroton. His brother Jack won the golf championship at Spring Lake when he was about 20. Dick said, "I was the youngest, and I thought if I was going to stand out or get any attention, I had to either achieve or be a clown. In fact, I was probably a little bit of both."

Circumstances prevented Irene Dillon from having an obvious influence on her son. However, judging by Dick's childhood memories, both Irene Dillon and her son Dick seem to have been strong willed. "I was not a nice kid," he said. "I remember my mother when I was about nine, holding me, fully clothed, under a cold shower to dampen my temper. I remember her going to *Gone with the Wind* when it first came out, about 1939. I was supposed to go with her, and I threw one of my fits, and she walked out the door and left me. I was looking out the window, and I can still see her, walking across Ocean Avenue to go to the movies."

But Dick said of his mother, "I hardly knew her." In July of 1945, when Dick was eleven, his mother died of cancer after being bed-ridden for several months. To shield Dick from the trauma of his mother's final illness, John Dillon sent Dick away to Camp Arcadia in Watertown, NY, for the summer. The counselors there "were a great bunch of guys. My counselor happened to be Joe Paterno of Penn State. He was a wonderful guy. He had to come tell me that my mother died, and years later I saw him, and I said, 'Dick Dillon. You probably don't remember me.' And he said, 'How can I forget you? I had to tell you your mother died.' He was a lovely man."

By September 1945, of the three Dillon children, Dick was the only one still living in the family home. Dick's older brother Jack was already married. Dick's sister Renee who "was a good pal and took care of me," was 18 and beginning an independent life. John Dillon did not want Dick to be alone, so he sent his twelve-year-old son away to Coindre Hall, a Catholic boarding school in Huntington, Long Island.

"I remember the first night at Coindre Hall, we were seated in the study hall, and we were watching a movie. There were about 90 kids, and I am crying my eyes, my heart out. The Brothers of the Sacred Heart were tough, extremely tough. Corporal punishment was part of their method of operation. You played all these sports, and we could shower only once a week so you pushed the dirt down to the bottom of the bed when you got into bed at night. I remember one day I was in the men's room taking a whiz, and the kid next to me said, 'Hey, Dillon, did you win?' and I said, 'Yeah' and with that, a Brother came in and said, 'You two are talking. Against the wall tonight at 8:00.' You'd stand facing the wall in your pajamas with your arms folded, and about an hour later, they'd come and get you, bring you into the bathroom, put you up against the sink, take your pajama bottoms down, and whack your fanny. I was there for two years, seventh and eighth grades. I was a good athlete, a very good athlete, so I was treated with respect by the kids. It wasn't all that bad but it was pretty bad.

"Once, we played a football game against Hicksville, and I was playing offense and defense, and this big 'farmer,' one big sucker, got loose and came through the line. I was the only thing between him and the goal, and I tackled him, but I tackled him right at the knees and I dislocated my right shoulder. Brother Andrew, the football coach who had worked hard with me to become a passer, said 'Can you play?' I said, 'No,' and he said, 'Try throwing with your left arm. I'm going to put you in and have you throw with your left arm.' I think I just said this was not a very good idea and I didn't go back in. I was about twelve at the time. Coindre Hall was tough. Very tough. There were some nice guys, and it probably wasn't as bad as it sounds.

"When we were playing baseball, the Brothers said that anyone who hit a home run was going to get a quart of milk. That was a big deal because milk was in very short supply. I hit a home run, and it took a hell of a long time to get the quart of milk. Whether you went home for the weekend depended on the grades you got. I wasn't going to stay there for a weekend so I was first in my class. I always HATED school, so the school had to be bad for me to be first in the class."

1947 was a pivotal year. Dick completed his two years at Coindre Hall. His father married Betty Johnston the same year, and they moved to an apartment on Park Avenue in Manhattan. About the same time, they sold the summer house in Long Branch and bought one in Spring Lake, New Jersey. Uncle Chubby and the aunts, Nellie and Hank, who had helped to raise Dick, "were thrown out" of the family home in Brooklyn when their sister Irene died. Dick's father knew about Canterbury School, a lay Catholic boarding school in New Milford, Connecticut, through his New York Catholic friends. He took Dick to Canterbury to meet Headmaster Dr. Nelson Hume, Dick was accepted, and that was it. At fourteen, Dick started at Canterbury in September of 1947.

CHAPTER TWO

CANTERBURY SCHOOL: 1947–1951

According to Dick, Canterbury School was "heaven" after Coindre Hall. "I remember the first day at Canterbury well. My sister took me to Grand Central Station and from there, the train took me into that little station in New Milford. On the bus from the station to the campus was this red-headed guy who had on a green suit. That was Michael Duffy and we became very good friends. We had to dress in coat and tie, and my ties were wild patterns, hand-me-downs from my father. Upper formers Neil Walsh, Frank McGuire, and David Cassidy conspired to dress me properly and sent me to Brooks Brothers to get me the proper clothes.

"I had a nice private room in North House dorm, now called Duffy House. Across from me was a Cuban, Mario Lobo. Canterbury was a very different experience from Coindre Hall for me, a very elegant experience. I remember dinner very vividly. We wore coat and tie for sit-down dinners with the faculty, and we had Filipino waiters."

Dick's first year at Canterbury was Headmaster Dr. Nelson Hume's last. He died in June of 1948, at the end of Dick's Third Form year. Dick saw Dr. Hume mostly as "a stern disciplinarian. When he'd walk down one of the paths, if you were going down and he was coming up, you'd want to get out of the way. You didn't want to fool with him. You wanted to be a good boy. Although he was quite a guy, he was so far above us that it was hard to relate to him, as opposed to some of the teachers. Mrs. Hume was a sweet lady, but by the time I was a student, they were not involved day by day."

Dick's positive description of Canterbury obscures the fact that academics were not Dick's strong suit. In fact, Dick's memory and his declaration that he HATED academics coincides with correspondence from Canterbury archives in which second headmaster Walter Sheehan and John Dillon communicated fairly frequently about how to work together to improve Dick's grades. Dick comments, "I think I had ADD. I remember at Canterbury a teacher was teaching, and I'm not paying any attention, just

7

looking out the window, daydreaming, and he reamed me up one side and down the other, which he had every right to do, but that's the way I was."

What did make Canterbury "like heaven" were the relationships forged with specific teachers and coaches, his friendships with other students, and his success in baseball and football and other aspects of the school such as theater. Dick especially singled out faculty members Frank Fisher and football coach Roger DesRoches. "Roger DesRoches was very important. He kind of took me under his wing. We had very good teams when Roger was coach. Frank was a heroic figure for me. It was very important to me at that point that he took an interest in me. Frank was the coach of junior varsity baseball and very few freshmen in the history of the School played junior varsity. They had to start out at the lower level and work their way up. I was the starter catcher on the junior varsity. I love to tell the story about Dr. Hume coming out to watch a baseball game, and I was at bat. I heard Dr. Hume say to Frank, 'Frank, that young man doesn't know how to hold a bat. Teach him how.' Frank said, 'Wait a minute, Dr. Hume,' and with that I literally lashed a ball to left center field for a double." Frank Fisher was also Dick's math teacher for two years, while Roger DesRoches was a mentor and friend--albeit a demanding coach--both on and off the field.

Dick was a student in the classes of other legendary teachers of the time: Lindman, Brodie, Mack, Koenig. "They were all great teachers, but kind of austere. All these guys rightfully liked the hard-working, successful student, and I was hard-working but not very successful. I didn't have the relationship with them that I did with DesRoches and Fisher. I loved Jean Hebert. He was rough and tough with me, but he was a lovable guy. He was an inspiration because he got mad at me one day and said, 'There's no way in hell you're going to get into Princeton, Dick.' And that kind of lit a fire under me."

The Tabard, Canterbury's school newspaper, verifies Dick's success in athletics, theater, and as a member of the community. In the fall of 1950, under the headline "Dillon Injured," a sports columnist wrote, "It has been Dillon's spirit and drive that have sparked the play of the Canterbury line in all pre-season workouts." Other articles mention his "fine defensive play." In December of 1950, the School produced the play *The Ghost Train,* and *The Tabard* reported, "The starring roles were many, but Dick Dillon, as Teddie Deakin, really deserved top billing for his performance. As a Scotland Yard man on the trail of the smugglers, and as a slightly annoying but happy English personage, Dick's acting was outstanding." This early, successful venture into theater laid the foundation for Dick's later participation in theater when the Dillons lived in Mexico.

Evidence that "Dill" was not just a jock who could act is that at graduation on June 2, 1951, Dick was given the Michael Burke Award: "To that boy who, through his zeal in all phases of endeavor, contributed much to the life of the School."

The influence of his father continues to be strong during Dick's Canterbury years. Dick commented that his brother Jack, as the oldest, was the favored son. Therefore, Dick was highly motivated to prove himself to his father. Definitely an involved father, John Dillon came to Canterbury to watch Dick in both football and baseball games, and he and Betty came up to see Dick perform in *The Ghost Train*. I asked Dick about his father's reaction to Dick's performance in the play. "Very positive," he said. "He cried." After watching Dick, in a baseball game against Trinity-Pawling, come around third base to score and collide with the catcher, his father commented, "Wow. You're getting tough, you know."

John Dillon also paid close attention to Dick's academic performance. The correspondence between Head Walter Sheehan and John Dillon during Dick's Canterbury years contains several refrains. Walter Sheehan's recurring point is, "the faculty feel he could do much better" but that "he is a good boy and we enjoy having him around." Dick's father's side of the correspondence contains such comments as, "I shall leave no stone unturned to get the desired results and if Dick fails to realize the opportunity that is his, we will have to take other steps to awaken him." However, this hard line took a different turn after Walter Sheehan stated that Dick was no "ball of fire scholastically" and not "Phi Beta timber." Tactfully but firmly, John Dillon responded, "I feel if we were to stay away from an I.Q. discussion, and if the teachers would occasionally give Dick a little pep talk, it might have better results. . . I have endeavored to impress him with the fact that regardless of any I.Q. rating, he has a lot on the ball, and with constant application he can achieve the success we expect of him."

By Dick's Fifth Form year, Sheehan reported that as a result of some testing, it seemed that ". . for years Dick has been going along with a reading disability, and to some extent undoubtedly that accounts for his failure to do better. . ." Years later, in the 1980s, as a Canterbury Trustee, Dick Dillon was instrumental in connecting Canterbury's administration with Dr. Peter Mueller, an expert in learning disabilities, and Dick advocated for incorporating knowledge about learning disabilities into Canterbury's approach in the classroom.

Walter Sheehan's final, formal evaluation of Dick Dillon was a recommendation for admission to Princeton, which said in part: "He has a good sense of humor and has proved to be a reliable boy with a sense of honor. . . In general, he has given the School a fine lift through his activities. In view of his fine improvement scholastically these past two years and the soundness of purpose he has shown about his work and about Princeton, I can recommend him highly to you."

"I always liked to work, to be active," Dick said at one point when he was discussing his dislike for academics. During his Canterbury years, he held a *Herald Tribune* franchise, and sold newspapers to Canterbury students. He worked for two summers on an ice delivery route, which came about through his Spring Lake friend Buddy Schock. "We were sitting in the kitchen of his home one summer, and we were wondering what we were going to do that summer. Both of us wanted to work. Buddy's father said, 'I have this old barge that I bought. I'll give you the barge, won't charge you, and an old truck I have, won't charge you, and you buy your ice and bait from me and service the fishing boats on the Manasquan River. So we used to go to work at 4:00 a.m. and by 9:00 we'd have all the boats serviced so we'd go back to the country club and play 36 holes of golf, and then we'd go back to the barge and service the incoming boats after their day of fishing. We made lots of money. My stepmother, one day when I came home, said, 'Dickie, I made your bed and there were two thousand dollars under your mattress.' I said, 'Yeah, I'm the treasurer.' My father thought that was great. He loved it. We did that job for two summers."

Dick's working partner from Spring Lake, Buddy Schock, became a lifelong friend. Dick said, "We were inseparable. He was like a brother." Buddy was best man at Dick and Phyllis's wedding. Bill Simon, a future Secretary of the Treasury, was also a Spring Lake friend. "He was about five or six years older than I, but very funny, very likable. He was kind of the overweight buffoon. Certainly not book smart." Their early acquaintance deepened into a firm friendship later during the 1970s.

During the summers at Spring Lake, Dick's father often invited important people to the house, including Richard Nixon and Nixon's friend Elmer Bobst of Warner-Lambert, after whom NYU's Bobst Library is named. Dick remembers one particular incident when his father had guests for breakfast, and Dick arrived home from working the boats. "One of the things we used to sell was a product called chum, ground up fish in ten gallon cans. It smelled like hell. That morning, I happened to fall in a bucket of chum and I smelled like hell. I walked in the house, and my father said, 'Dickie, come sit down for breakfast with my pals here.' I said, 'Dad, I smell like fish.' But he said, 'Sit down.' So I sat next to this woman, and she finally turned green, and I was excused. My father wasn't particularly demonstrative, but I think he was proud of me."

When Dick went home to Manhattan from Canterbury for the holidays, he would have arranged dates, and he would meet the dates under the clock at the Biltmore. Somehow Headmaster Walter Sheehan discovered this: "He kind of singled me out as an unserious playboy. He called me "the Ghost of the Biltmore." One of Dick's experiences during his Sixth Form year fed this impression. With the earnings Dick made from the ice barge and his *Tribune* franchise, he went to Bermuda for Easter. There, he met an attractive young woman, and in an attempt to impress her, he "fibbed" and told her he was a freshman at Brown University. Back at Canterbury after the break, as students gathered in North House for mail distribution one day, Walter Sheehan announced with sarcasm, "Here is a letter addressed to Brown Boy. Oh, Dillon, you're the Brown Boy?"

The *Cantuarian,* Canterbury's yearbook, corroborated Dick's story about the Biltmore. The Class Prophecy in the 1951 yearbook contained the following, ". . I regarded a beautiful yacht with candy striped orange and black sails, which, I later found out, belonged to "Richee" Dillon, the New York playboy. The amazing feature of this craft is that it has a perfect reproduction of the Biltmore Lounge. . ." On the other hand, the yearbook also supported Dick's statement that he was hard-working. The list of superlatives for his class included the line, "Hardest worker: Dillon, Chapelle."

Canterbury introduced Dick to some cultures and attitudes that were not part of his Brooklyn upbringing. "I don't know if you want to hear this story," Dick said with a wry grin. "This guy went home for Christmas during my first year and when we came back, he says, 'What'd you get?' And I said, 'Oh, I got a Brooks blazer and a catcher's mitt. Good stuff. What did you get?' 'My father gave me a charge account at the local whore house,' he said. The kid was 14 years old! Very, very wealthy and from Latin America."

Several Canterbury friendships were rich and enduring ones. The boy in the green suit from Dick's very first day, Michael Duffy, became a lifelong friend. They attended Princeton together, and after Michael became a Maryknoll father, Phyllis and Dick stayed in touch while he was in Tanzania and later in Ossining, NY. He visited the Dillons in Mexico, Newport Beach, and New York, and he officiated at the Dillons' daughter Patty's wedding. Dick wrote Michael's obituary for the Princeton weekly.

Tony Alexandre was also a good Canterbury friend who went on to Princeton with Dick and Michael. Tony and Michael were ushers at Phyllis and Dick's wedding. Mario Lobo, the Cuban boy who lived across the hall from Dick in his first year, invited Dick and Phyllis to Cuba for an unforgettable vacation in 1959. Peter Eigo, another lifelong friend, started as a Third Former with Dick, but graduated a year later because of illness during his Fifth Form year. John Smith was in the class behind Dick and attended Canterbury for only a year, but he and his wife were key contacts during the years the Dillons were in Mexico. Classmate Bob Holmen was an important business contact when Dick owned Mendoza Dillon, his advertising company. Dick and Peter Carney, Canterbury class of '50 and Princeton alumnus, established a post-Canterbury relationship that continued on to fishing trips in Montana in 2015 and after.

Dick's father never lost sight of the fact that his goal for Dick at Canterbury was acceptance at Princeton. "My father had a fifth grade education, and he really wanted his sons to go to Princeton." Early in Dick's final year at Canterbury, he told his father that he'd like to think about going to a college other than Princeton. "I wanted to continue to play football and baseball, and I thought I had a much better chance at a smaller college like Williams or Amherst. This was big. Dad's reply was, 'Great. Go wherever you want. The only place where I pay the bills is Princeton.' End of discussion."

On May 8, 1951, Dick called his father to report that he had been admitted to Princeton University. On June 2, 1951, Richard Emmett Dillon graduated from Canterbury School. His father, step-mother Betty, sister Irene and her fiancé, and brother Jack and his wife attended the ceremony. And so begins a new chapter in Dick's life.

Lou Mandler

CHAPTER THREE

FROM PRINCETON TO THE ARMY: 1951–1956

Dick carried his father's expectations with him to Princeton. "My father was really happy when I got into Princeton. My brother was a ne'er do well and got thrown out of there. He was a terrific guy, a great sense of humor, terrific golfer, and I loved him, but he didn't take anything very seriously. I didn't want to be what he was."

Dick's athletic goals were initially realized at Princeton. "I played 150 pound football. I was the guard and Don Rumsfeld was the tackle. We became very good friends. Then I broke my ankle in my junior year. I remember Rumsfeld was out for some reason, and he threw me over his shoulder and carried me up to the infirmary." Dick would connect again with Rumsfeld in the years between Rumsfeld's terms as Secretary of Defense.

Dick also played freshman baseball. "I was a walk-on, the starting second baseman. We had our last intra-squad game on a Thursday before opening against Yale that Saturday, and I had a pick-off at second base. I didn't get my hand out of the way, and the guy came and spiked my right hand, and it blew up, and that was the end of baseball for me. At that point there were so many good players that with an injury like that, you're done. You're fried. The guy who spiked my hand, John Sienkewicz, became a close friend."

Dick's struggle with academics continued at Princeton. "I had to work twice as hard as anyone else in order to succeed. And I did." As was true before and after Canterbury, Dick had a vibrant social life at Princeton. His two roommates, Danny Lane and Dozier Garner, were part of Phyllis and Dick's wedding party. Dick belonged to the Cap and Gown eating club of which Canterbury alumnus Peter Carney was president. When members of the Cottage eating club took a suite of rooms and needed two more students to fill out the suite, they invited Dick and Bill Yort from the Cap and Gown club, and the group became known as the Cottage Cap and Gown Suite.

Towards the end of Dick's freshman year, in April of 1952, Phyllis Freschi entered his life. "One day, I came out of lunch with Bill Ruckelshaus, who later became Attorney General, and Tommy Pettus, who died young, and Pettus said to us, 'You and Rucky have to come up to Yale with me for junior prom this weekend.' I said, 'You probably have a date, and we don't.' Pettus said he would fix us up so we go up. Pettus introduced us to our blind dates, and it was not a good show. So Rucky and I climbed out a window and ran away. We wandered around the Yale campus for a while until about 10:00 when we came upon this club and saw our friend Howie Price dancing with a pretty blond. I cut in and introduced myself, and we went through the 'Where did you go to school' and all that.

"Then I said, 'I could never fall in love with you.'

"She said, 'Why not?'

"You're too tall," I said.

"She went over to the side, took off her high heeled shoes, and that was history. And then my future wife dumped me in sophomore year and most of junior year."

Phyllis Freschi was born in Cleveland to Burnette ("Boots") Billman and Lou Knighten. Lou was thirteen years older than Burnette and had courted her while he was working in New York, and she was attending Smith College. They had been married about a year when Lou was killed in an automobile accident. Boots then moved back to her mother's house in St. Louis with Phyllis, her infant daughter. She went back to school to get her degree and, afterwards, taught school in a one-room schoolhouse.

Phyllis's Grandmother and Grandfather Billman were like parents to her. Phyllis remembered, "Grandmother's house was just beautiful. My granddaddy had a quarry, and he built the house and all the walls around it. They had tennis courts and horses. It was a gentleman's farm with chickens and horses and cows. I learned how to milk a cow, and we churned the milk to make butter. It was just an idyllic childhood. Every Sunday there was a gathering of Billmans; there were three girls, my mother and two sisters.

"I remember when Mother met Dad--or Googy, as we called him--I was about 5 or 6 years old. When they came back from their honeymoon, he adopted me. My grandparents gave my mother and Googy the carriage house that was attached to their house, and that's where I grew up. The horses were down there and that's how I came to love horses. It was an incredible life style. Googy was in the pasta business; Raverino and Freschi spaghetti was one of the top brands in the United States. His parents and uncles came from Italy and started the company. My mother then had six children with Googy. I am seven years older than their first child."

Phyllis and her six siblings have maintained a close family connection throughout the years. Phyllis and her three sisters meet annually for three or four days of talking, shopping, eating, and theater. In an arrangement set up by their parents, all seven siblings meet every Easter for two weeks in two units of the Marriott Camelback in Scottsdale, Arizona.

"I went to high school at Villa Duchesne in St. Louis; I was a good Sacred Heart child. After high school, my mother said I should go east to school so I went to Marymount in Tarrytown, and I majored in men's colleges. In the process, I met Dick. I was with a friend of his, and he cut in on me.

"I met his family that spring. We'd go into the city for the day. He was driving me all around in his Cadillac, and I remember going to his parents' apartment on Park Avenue. Here was this Sacred Heart girl, and I don't know anything about New York. They had help all over the place and fingerbowls and waiters. Our cultural backgrounds were very different. The Irish, Dick's family, was more nouveau. They came from nothing, and you could tell they came from nothing, but they had everything, and my family had always had something. We were easy with it; it was more of a lifestyle. It was very, very different. I used to tell Dick, 'You don't know anything about Oriental rugs; you don't know anything about great music.' My grandparents used to take me to the opera and the symphony; those were important. For Dick's family the important thing was to go to the 21 Club.

"His father was an over-the-top kind of person—big, big, huge personality. I was somewhat intimidated by him. My mother used to call him 'a most lovable bastard.' I kind of felt sorry for Betty. I met all their family and all their kids, and I'm still close to them. I loved his brother Jack and I loved his sister Renee. She was quite a personality. They were quick witted, always joking. I never met Uncle Chubby and I met the aunts only once. Dick and his family were distanced from them. Maybe Popsy thought people were using him. He was quite wealthy and they weren't.

"Their relationship with their family was nothing like mine. When I was growing up we used to go to Nona and Poppy's house for dinner every

Sunday. She was an incredible, incredible cook. The aunts and uncles would all come, and we all had jobs. Mine was to grind the coffee. She made minestrone, a curry, saffron rice with veal. After dinner, the men would go into the living room and listen to the opera, the Texaco opera. They all could sing all those songs. Dad sang until his dying day. Dick got to one of those dinners, and he loved it.

"After my freshman year at Marymount, New York, my mother wanted me to come back to St. Louis, so I graduated from Marymount in St. Louis. Dick and I were freshmen when we met, and we didn't get married until we graduated; it was rocky along the way. I had other interests. There was a guy, a polo player, who asked me to exercise his horses, which I loved doing. He would come over to the barn after I had finished with the horses and ask me to go out to dinner. He gave me a ring when I was a junior, but I only told my grandmother and Dick. Dick said, 'Great. You're doing what you want to do. We have a house party weekend coming up, and you've always enjoyed a good party, so why don't you come up for a last hurrah?'

"When I got off the plane after that weekend, my mother looked at me and said, 'You're in love.' I said, 'He wants to get engaged this summer, but I told him that you don't want to be engaged your whole senior year. Nobody wants to be engaged senior year. You want to be free.' But my mother said, 'You'll get engaged this summer!' She didn't like this other guy for me, and she was right."

Dick said of the other guy, "I used to call him a Nazi. He was about twelve years older than Phyllis and he preyed on young women."

Phyllis concluded, "So I called Dick and said, 'When you come, bring a ring.' So we were engaged through senior year."

In June 1955, Dick graduated from Princeton on a Tuesday, received an army commission as a lieutenant in artillery that Wednesday, and got married that Saturday. Buddy Schock was best man, and Mike Duffy and Tony Alexandre were ushers. Dick and Phyllis had a long honeymoon in Acapulco, where they ran into Billy Mellon, a Princeton classmate of Dick's, and John Smith, a former Canterbury student. A few years later, they would encounter John again in Mexico.

Back in New York, Dick and Phyllis moved into his father's apartment on Fifth Avenue, and then Dick's father sent them off to Wisconsin and other places for a few weeks to learn the printing business. This was during the World Series so they listened to baseball games all the way.

On October 1, 1955, Dick reported to camp as a 2nd lieutenant at Fort Sill in Oklahoma. College graduates could be commissioned, and Dick had done two years of ROTC at Princeton. Although the Korean War ended in 1954, the draft was still in effect. Other Princeton friends, David Amory and Joe Castle, were also at Fort Sill, and they spent much time at the Dillon house. Phyllis said, "I didn't know how to make a cup of coffee. I could open a can of corned beef hash and put an egg on top of it. David Amory gave me some cooking lessons, and I read cookbooks. My mother had given me my grandmother's cookbook."

After three months at Fort Sill, Dick was assigned to Fort Benning, Georgia, the Third Infantry Division. He started "at the bottom of the food chain" as a forward observer (sees the enemy and radios back) and worked his way up to fire direction center (sees the ground, gives the elevation) and then became the battery executive officer (coordinates the two). "This was a good position for a rookie lieutenant. I loved getting out of academics to something practical and active, and I wanted to be successful. It was my first exposure to the real world. The artillery battery, which is the same as a company in the infantry, had 250 men. The sergeants, who are the guts of the army, were all veterans of the Second World War and Korea. I thought I was doing pretty well."

For Phyllis, Fort Benning was "exciting and fun. I was never lonely. Major Davis and his wife Mary kind of adopted us. Mother would come to visit and bring my sisters. One Sunday, we went to church and saw Peter Eigo from Canterbury and discovered he and his wife Tricia were at Fort Benning. Tricia was the sister of Des Barry, another Canterbury alum. We became inseparable. I named my daughter Patricia because of Tricia Eigo. At one point, Tricia was pregnant, I was pregnant, and my mother was pregnant."

In April of 1956, Dick and Phyllis's first child, Richard, was born at Fort Benning in a military hospital. "It was a horrible experience," said Phyllis. "I had been out walking with a civilian friend, and when I came back and got in the car, I was in a puddle of water. I knew nothing. When I got home, Dick was there, and he told me to call my friend Judy. I said to her, 'What do I do now?'

"Call the hospital," she said.

"They told me to come in, and when we got there, they put me in this big room where there were fifteen other women in labor. Dick couldn't stay with me so he went to the Davises for dinner. I remember being in a corner and listening to the screaming and yelling, and every time someone would scream, the doctor would come in, and then they would scream louder. I tore those sheets to ribbons and said fifteen thousand rosaries. I just wasn't going to make a sound.

"Finally, a nurse came by and said, 'What's going on with you?' She looked at me, and said, 'Dear God, you're about to deliver this baby! Get up and go to the bathroom!'

"I said, 'I can't!'

"She said, 'Yes, you can. Get up and go the bathroom.' So you do it. Then they bring the cart in and they said, 'Get up and get on the cart.'

"I said, 'I can't.'

"Yes, you can. Get up and get on the cart!" Then you get into the operating room.

"Get up and get on the table." I'm telling you it was a good thing it was my first child because I had no idea what was going on. So I got off the cart and got on the table and the next thing I knew, I had this child. I produced a child.

"I was really lucky because there was one private room that the General's wife had been in, and she had just moved out. There were no beds elsewhere so I had the room all to myself. Every morning they would bring in clean sheets and say, 'Get up and change your sheets.' I had a stack of clean sheets this tall under my bed by the time I left.

"Dickie was really little. He weighed about five pounds. They didn't tell you not to smoke or drink then. I didn't do that much, but I think I smoked and did a little of both throughout the pregnancy, and I often wondered whether that stunted his growth. He was a beautiful baby, beautiful. When Patty was born the next year, we could get our own doctor, and I had a divine doctor who wore Brooks Brothers suits. That was a totally different story."

Not long after Richard's birth, Dick had an experience that was the core of the graduation address he gave to Canterbury students in June, 2014. In the talk titled, "The Positive Power of Failure," Dick said, "The army experience changed my life. It has been said that humiliation is the single most powerful emotion, and overcoming humiliation is the second most powerful one. After the army, I no longer had a fear of failure. The positive power of failure was an important factor in my journey through the maze of life."

CHAPTER FOUR

THE ARMY: 1956–1957

During Dick's time in the Army, he encountered or served under veterans from World War II and the Korean War. Especially notable among them were William A. ("Wild Bill") Harris and Robert Frederick Sink.

Harris received the Distinguished Service Cross for extraordinary heroism in the Korean War as Commanding Officer of the 7th Cavalry Regiment, 1st Cavalry Division. The saddle and Gary Owen insignia evident in photos of the time evoke thoughts of George Armstrong Custer, another memorable general of the 7th Cavalry. Harris received several more awards, the last being the Army Distinguished Service Medal in 1966. In his book *Marching On,* Gordon Sumner, Jr. says of Harris, "Describing this man as 'colorful' is an understatement." Harris retired as a U.S. Army Major General.

Sink began his post-West Point career in 1927 as a Second Lieutenant at Fort Screven, Georgia. Throughout World War II, he commanded the 506th Parachute Infantry Regiment in Europe. At the beginning of the Korean War, he was assistant commander of the Seventh Infantry Division in Korea, and was subsequently given numerous commands ranging from Fort Campbell, Kentucky to Fort Bragg, North Carolina. In 1958, he became Commander, Strategic Army Corps (SAC), United States Army.

Dick counts his army years as perhaps the most formative experience of his adult life. As he tells it: "One day my whole company went out to the boondocks somewhere for a field exercise with all the personnel and guns. My responsibility as the battery executive officer was to find a place to put the guns, 105mm Howitzers. Sergeant Griffin was one of the veterans from the Second World War—Normandy--and Korea. I liked the guy. We were walking through the woods looking for a place for the guns, and he was kind of mumbling to himself. I said, 'Sergeant Griffin, what's the matter?'

"He said, 'Nothing, nothing.'

"He kept mumbling, and I said, 'What the hell is going on?'"

"He said, 'Lieutenant, if I told you, you'd court martial me.'"

"I said, 'Well, who's going to be the witnesses? The birds and the bees and the squirrels? Come on!'"

"So then he said, 'Lieutenant, we think you're the biggest son of a bitch in the United States Army.'"

"My God. My jaw dropped. I'm twenty-two years old, and I didn't say anything else. We went back to the staging area where the rest of the battery was. There were big trucks with the guns attached and the troops in the back, and in the cab of each truck were a private driver and one of the NCOs (non-commissioned officers) next to him. I gave the hand signal to rev up and move out, and I looked in the cab of one of these trucks, and the driver and the NCO were flipping me the bird.

"I was devastated. The field commission captain, McDonald, came out and told me to get in the Jeep and go to headquarters and see the colonel. The colonel told me to get my wife and child and take off for two weeks and then come back. Nobody ever really explained it to me, but I guess there were two things. First, who was I, and who was I dealing with? Captain McDonald disliked Ivy Leaguers. He and the first sergeant, Patrick, who was his right arm, were cut from the same cloth. They were pretty foul-mouthed people and pretty rough around the edges, and I certainly think their feeling about Ivy Leaguers had an influence. Second, I guess I was arrogant. I guess I didn't give commands in the right voice and wasn't as conscious of the emotions of the troops as I should have been, but there was no evidence of mutiny from the unit. Anyway, that's what happened.

"So Phyllis and I and Dickie went to my parents' house in Spring Lake, New Jersey, and had a delightful time with the family on the beach. I tried to let the incident roll off me. When we went back and went through the gates at Fort Benning, I said, 'The bad news is that it happened. The good news is that I'll get a new start.' They put me back in the same unit and demoted me. They didn't take my butter bar which is the gold bar that lieutenants have, but I went from battery executive officer to forward observer.

"I was down at the bottom of the food chain again and started working my way back up. The best thing that happened was Captain McDonald moved on, and a new guy came in. He liked me and after about three months, he moved me up. Then he left, and another one came in, and he liked me, and when he left, he recommended that I become the commanding officer of the unit. This was about six months after the incident. The first thing I did when I took over as commander of the unit was to get rid of Sergeant Patrick, Captain McDonald's right arm. He was not a nice man, and it felt good.

"I put in one of the veterans from the unit as first sergeant. His name was Snuffy Hoffman because he chewed snuff. He was terrible. He'd spit and get it all over his uniform. It was pretty funny. My immediate superior, the colonel, knew I loved Snuffy. He'd call me and say, 'Dick, I'm bringing some visitors to your unit. Put Snuffy in the closet, will you?'

"I'd say to Snuffy, 'You know what that's about, don't you?'

"He'd say, 'Yeah, I'll go in the closet.'

"He was a wonderful man. One day we had an inspector general inspection, which in peacetime is a big deal. That's when Washington sends down a big group of men, officers and sergeants, to inspect the division of 20,000 men. It would take about two weeks to comb through every single unit in the Third Infantry Division. When they got through, they named the winning, best-run unit in the division. Snuffy, as first sergeant, got our unit in perfect shape for the inspection. We were named the top unit, and Snuffy made it happen. We had to parade before the general and the colonels, and we got a trophy. Here I am out in front of the troops as a commander, and when I got back to my office with Snuffy, here were all the NCOs, who had pooh-poohed on me six months before, waiting to tell me how much they loved me. We were written up in the army newspaper called *Stars and Stripes*. This was a seminal point in my life.

"Another time, General Lindquist, who was the two-star commanding general of the Third Infantry Division, called down to the colonel who called down to me to say, 'Dick, General Lindquist is coming down, and he wants to talk to you. Get your troops ready. Put Snuffy in the closet.'

"We were in a part of Fort Benning that had old World War II barracks. When General Lindquist saw them, he said, 'I want to show the army what can be done with these old barracks. I want you to put up plywood walls, plywood ceilings, paint them, get some curtains in.'

"I said, 'I'd be honored to do this, but I'll need some money to get this done.'

"The general said, 'Get your budget together and call my aide.' So I got my budget together and called the aide, and the aide would never talk to me, and the general would never talk to me, so I went to the colonel and said, 'I think I'm getting screwed.'

"He said, 'You're right on. Go talk to General Harris.' So I went to see General Harris, and he said, 'Dick, you're screwed. I can't help you. You're going to have to figure something else out.'

"So I went back to the unit and told Snuffy about it. He said, 'Don't worry. I can take care of this.'

"I said, 'Come on!'

"He said, 'No, I can. Close your eyes. Relax. It'll be done in two weeks.'

"At night Snuffy took big trucks and ran paint. I don't know how the hell he collected it, but he went over to the main campus of Fort Benning, and he took plywood off the walls of the barracks over there and brought it back. Totally unorthodox. Totally. Incredible. He painted, the wives of the NCOs and Phyllis made curtains, and we made the deadline. Lindquist was absolutely enthralled. Snuffy was incredible. We were written up in the *Stars and Stripes* again saying how great we were.

"From there, it was all good. I worked with my troops for probably another three months and then I was promoted to the battalion to be in planning and operations. I was there about two days when the colonel brought me to his office and said, 'General Harris (the artillery general division commander) wants you to be his aide. Go up and see him.' That's a big deal, big deal.

"Do I have to buy new clothes and stuff?" I asked.

"He laughed and said, 'No, we'll get you some braids and insignia to put on your arm.'

"General Harris was West Point, a Korea veteran, and a character. They called him Wild Bill Harris because when he was in Korea commanding the 1st Cavalry, he would ride around with a saddle on his Jeep with a big red light and a siren. He was from an old army family, and most of those old army families start out with the cavalry. We had a wonderful time. As his aide, I didn't do a heck of a lot. I sat right outside his office. He had a driver and a car and would pick me up in the morning and take me all over. He was a great guy.

"Years later, when we were living in Mexico, General Billy came to see us, and he did something that showed what kind of a guy he was. At the time, one of my Princeton friends, Peter Millard, was visiting us. Peter's father and General Billy had graduated from West Point in the same class, 1933. Peter's father died in a plane accident shortly after Peter was born so Peter never really knew him. After General Billy met Peter in Mexico, he went back to the States, contacted other West Point classmates, collected memorabilia about Peter's father, put together a scrapbook, and sent it to Peter.

"One day, General Billy said to me, 'Go home and get your stuff. We're going to Fort Bragg. General Sink, the commanding general of Fort Bragg, is coming in on his private plane and we'll fly to Bragg with him.' Sink was a three-star general, Harris was a one-star, and I was a butter bar. On the plane, Sink, who was a big bridge player, said, 'Come on, Dillon, you're a fourth in bridge.' He was a big boozer. We had a raucous time.

"When we got to Bragg, Sink told Harris that we would stay at his house, not the officer's quarters as we expected. At his house, Sink said to me, 'OK, Dick, do you know anyone at Bragg that you'd like to have dinner with us?'

"I said, 'Yeah, there's a guy from Princeton; we were in the same club—G. Gibson Carey, the Third.'

"Wait here," he said. He made a phone call and then said, "G. Gibson Carey, the Third will be here in about five minutes. Meet him at the front door."

"Gibby came up the walk brushing his hair and making sure his uniform was all right. He didn't know what the hell was going on. I opened the door and he almost fainted.

This was the same Sink that was in the *Band of Brothers* that is currently still on the air; it tells of the exploits of E Company of the 101st Airborne Division in Normandy. After dinner, we sat in his living room, and everyone told war stories. It was fabulous.

"General Harris wanted me to stay in the army, and I took a test to mollify him. I scored very high, but my six year old could have scored high. When he talked to me about staying in the army, I said, 'General Billy, you know I sit outside your office, and I can hear you on the phone. You can't pay your insurance, and I don't want to live like that. I've got to get out and go into business.' He understood that.

Our daughter Patty was born in May of 1957, and in October of 1957, I got out of the army, honorably discharged. I was twenty-three years old with a wife and two children, and I didn't really know what I wanted to do.

"The army experience taught me that failure is not fatal. It is the courage to continue that counts. The army gave me great confidence because I had been knocked down and almost knocked out. And I came up from the floor and I won. That was a tremendous experience. After that, there is little you can't do."

Dick's First Communion at Holy Innocent Church.

Dick at the Dillon Long Branch, New Jersey summer home, about 1941

Renee, Dick, Irene O'Hara Dillon, and John Dillon about 1944

Coindre Hall Grade 8 graduation photo, 1947. Dick is in the middle row, second from the right end. To the left of Dick is a Ronzoni of the spaghetti Ronzonis. Vin Cashman, uncle of Brian Cashman, is first person in the second row.

Dick in front of the Canterbury chapel.
Fall 1947.

THE MIMERS

PRESENT

THE GHOST TRAIN

BY

ARNOLD RIDLEY

With the following Cast of Characters
(In order of Appearance)

Richard Winthrop	Antony Smith
Elsie Winthrop	Joseph Burns
Saul Hodgkin	John Queenan
Charles Murdock	Herbert McLaughlin
Peggy Murdock	John Shaw
Miss Bourne	Terrence Canavan
Teddie Deakin	Richard Dillon
John Price	Joseph Walsh
Herbert Price	Morgan Murray
John Sterling	Daniel Wilson
Jackson	Brenton Fuger

The action of the play takes place in the waiting room
of the Railway Station at Clear Vale Junction, on a branch
line near Rockland, Maine

ACT I. At ten thirty, P. M.

ACT II. At eleven fifteen, P. M.

ACT III. Midnight

Program for "The Ghost Train" listing Dick
as Teddie Deakin. Fall 1950.

Canterbury's Third Form, 1947-1948. Dick Dillon and Mario Lobo, back row. Tony
Alexandre and Michael Duffy, front row.

Canterbury's Varsity Football team. Dick is first on the left in the front row. Roger DeRoches is at the extreme right in the third row.

Canterbury's varsity baseball team. Dick is second from the right in the front row. Headmaster and coach Walter Sheehan is the extreme left in the middle row.

Dick with friends Bruce Newman, Joanne Larkin, and Barbara Nugent at the Spring Lake, New Jersey beach.

Canterbury friends Ed Carey, Mario Lobo, Dick, and Cole with dates in a Manhattan club,

Phyllis and Dick Dillon's wedding.
June, 1955,

Dick with best man and Spring Lake friend
Buddy Schock.

Princeton friends, Back row, unidentified, Heiden, Dillon, Lane, Weyland, Yort, Gardner.

Left: Phyllis Freschi's 1952 debut with her mother Billie (Boots) Burnette Freschi and grandmother Brent Billman.

Below, left: Phyllis at the airport leaving for Mexico with four children on leashes. 1961.

Below, right: General Billy Harris during the Korean War.

Dillon clan about 1961. Taken as a gift for John Dillon's 60th birthday. Dick and Phyllis with Richard, Patty, Michael, and Stephen. Jack and Dolly Dillon with their four children, Betty Dillon, Renee and Jack Davis and their seven children.

Lou Mandler

CHAPTER FIVE

FROM J.C. DILLION PRINTING TO GENERAL FOODS IN MEXICO: 1957–1961

John Dillon, Dick's father, always a powerful figure in his life, determined the first step of Dick's career after his military service. Dick said, "After I got out of the army, I knew my father wanted and expected me to be part of his business. So I said to myself, 'I've got to give this a try.'

"We lived for about six months in the family house in Spring Lake, and I commuted to New York, about a two and a half hour commute each way. Then my brother called and said there was a little house for sale in Rye, New York. We loved it. It was $15,000. I didn't have any money so I had to borrow $3,000 from Phyllis's mother for a down payment because my father wouldn't give me any money. He had told me when I graduated from Princeton, 'I paid for your education. Don't ask me for any more money.' We moved to Rye and liked it very much."

Phyllis admits she viewed the idea of living in Rye with some trepidation. "Coming from St. Louis, I thought the whole Eastern seaboard was going to be very uppity. I was at sixes and sevens as far as friends. I was away from my family, so friends were really important. But people could not have been kinder or more welcoming. It was a great experience. An old friend from Spring Lake, Mary Carter, and a friend of mine from St. Louis, Helen Cooley, helped us make our first connections. In Rye, we formed probably the strongest friendships we've had—friends that have been our mainstay through going to Mexico and all the different places. Scott and Janice Pierce, Hugh and Nancy Beath, the Blumenthals were all very important.

"It was a clubby little town, but it was a really a wonderful, wonderful rich time for us. We had our little house on Hill Street, which Tricia Eigo helped us find, and we made our best friendships. Michael was born in Rye in 1958, and Stephen in 1959 so I had four little children during that time. I can't believe it now, but the children didn't seem to get in the way of our getting together with everyone. We all smoked and had air conditioning only in our bedroom. So the Pierces and the Dillons would sit in our bedroom with the air conditioner, just puffing away. I don't know why it didn't kill us all."

The Manursing Island Club in the summer gave both Phyllis and Dick the opportunity to play tennis, and winter excursions involved skiing in Vermont.

Dick's time in his father's company began well. "My first client when I worked for my father was Gene Reilly, my Canterbury English teacher who had left teaching to start a company dealing with television ratings. I always liked him. Later, when our son Bill was at Canterbury, Gene got me on Canterbury's board of trustees. I also got the Johnson and Johnson account for my father. But I couldn't stand working for my father. I loved him and admired him, but he was very dictatorial, and I would stand up to him. My father had his office on one side of the hall, and my brother on the other end. I would come out of my father's office after a fight, and I'd go into my brother's office and slam the door and say, 'Do you know what that old bastard just said to me?'

"Jack used to laugh like hell about it. He said, 'Then you'd walk out, and the old man would come in, slam the door, and say, 'Do you know what that little son of a bitch said?'

"I was successful there, but I wasn't happy. An incident in my first months there showed the internal conflict I was going through. My father took me to lunch with Daniel Norton, the president of Nestle U.S., and Ed Daley, the advertising manager. After lunch, my father told me to wait with Ed while he talked with Norton. In Ed's office, Ed said to me, 'What's wrong? You look so unhappy.' That my conflict was so obvious pushed me to make a decision about my future.

"After about six months, I came home to Phyllis and said, 'I can't do this for a living. I take these purchasing agents out to lunch, the only time they see the inside of a decent restaurant, have a couple martinis, three-hour lunches. I drink with them because I am expected to drink with them, but I don't want to drink with them. If I continue with this, I'm going to become an alcoholic.'

"She was totally supportive. She said, 'Go for it.' So I started to send out resumes, without my father's knowledge, and after another six months, I hit gold. A top executive at General Foods, which was then the largest food company in the United States, offered me a job for the same money that my father was paying me. So I went in and told my father. He said, 'What are they paying you?'

"I said, 'The same as you are.'

"You're lying," he said. Then he said, "You're never going to be able to afford a fur coat for your wife."

"I don't care and I don't think she does either," I said. "I just have to get out of here." My father was furious. He blamed Princeton and its high falutin ideas.

"I said, 'No, Dad, it was the army.' And with that, I left and started with General Foods. He eventually came around in a couple years, but he could never understand why I did these crazy things. I mean I married Phyllis, and he didn't approve of that. He didn't see that she was a great woman. He thought she was kind of wacky. My brother and sister were very proud of me for standing up to my father. My brother Jack was a lovely guy, but he drank too much, and his life was geared to booze and playthings. He was a great golfer. Jack did things that eventually killed the business."

In March of 1959, just before Dick left his father's company, he and Phyllis went to Cuba as guests of Dick's Canterbury classmate, Mario Lobo. Castro had overthrown the Batista government in January of that year, but the wealthy Lobo family remained in Cuba. At that point, their properties and sugar business were untouched by the new communist government. Mario's uncle, Julio Lobo, was considered the single most powerful sugar broker in the world. He owned fourteen sugar mills, hundreds of thousands of acres of land, a bank, and an insurance company with offices in Cuba, New York, London, Spain, and the Philippines. It wasn't until October, 1960, when Che' Guevara moved to nationalize Lobo's refineries and cane fields, that Lobo's empire collapsed. A 2010 book, *The Sugar King of Havana: The Rise and Fall of Julio Lobo, Cuba's Last Tycoon* by John Paul Rathbone, chronicles Lobo's life.

When Dick and Phyllis went to Cuba, Mario paid their way, gave them a Jaguar to use for the two weeks they were there, and hosted festive dinners every night. As Rathbone's book puts forth, the Lobos were an example of the Cuban bourgeoisie who initially supported the 1959 revolution for its nationalistic overtones. When discussing their Cuban visit, Phyllis said,

"Everyone at these dinners was for Castro except for Mario's wife. But at one dinner there was news that Castro had nationalized the TV stations."

Shortly after the Dillons' visit, Mario Lobo got out of Cuba after mailing money to an office in New York. He then lived in Vail, Colorado, where Phyllis and Dick later connected with him.

Dick related an amusing story originating from their Cuban visit. "We were living in Mexico in 1962, and we encountered a Cuban couple. The man told me that I looked familiar. It turned out he had had a cigar store in Havana in 1959, and I came in wearing shorts. Cubans didn't wear shorts, so I stood out." Another later coincidence is that a huge real estate property near the Dillons' home in Vero Beach is owned by Julio Lobo's daughter.

Dick's first position at General Foods was Export Manager for the Caribbean. As part of the job, he occasionally travelled to the Islands for two weeks at a time. "Phyllis would drive me in a blinding snow storm to Idlewild airport, as it was called then; I would get on the plane, flying first class and have a martini on the flight. Then I'd spend time on Island beaches. Phyllis had no idea of the luxury I enjoyed on those trips."

A significant accomplishment Dick remembered during this stint at General Foods was his involvement with marketing Tang, an orange-flavored drink concentrate. "The Island of Aruba was pretty non-productive as far as fruit goes at the time. I thought Tang might go over well there, and I recommended that General Foods spend quite a lot of money on a radio campaign for Tang. It was pooh-poohed at first, but eventually they did it, and it was successful."

Despite his success as Export Manager for the Caribbean and his appreciation for some of the perks of the job, Dick had higher goals: "I wanted an international experience because that was the fastest way to get to the top. General Foods had a couple companies that were focused on Mexico. We had been there on our honeymoon where I ran across John Smith, who had spent a year at Canterbury, married a wonderful Mexican gal, and had his career in Mexico. Our paths crossed pretty significantly while we were there.

"When Jorge Kovacs, the new head of General Foods in Mexico, would come to headquarters, I would make sure to see him and ingratiate myself to him. I told him I'd love to come down to Mexico to work for him. So I got an offer to work for a General Foods company called Rosa Blanca that made small packets of powdered consommé, which they sold in small outlets in Mexico where the majority of the poor population shopped. So off we went to Mexico."

The move to Mexico in 1961 was the first of many for Phyllis that involved finding and furnishing a house for the Dillon family, enrolling the children in schools, and settling into a new culture. For this first move, Dick had gone ahead, so she travelled alone from New York to Mexico with four children: Richard (6), Patty (5), Michael (4), and Stephen (3). Daughter Patty commented on the photo of Phyllis travelling with her four children: "Nothing ever rattles my mom—she just solves the problem. . . she had to navigate safely through international airports in the U.S. and Mexico—why not just put them all on leashes? Meanwhile, she looks fabulous, very glamorous with her perfectly done hair and heels and swing coat. . and four kids on leashes!"

This equanimity seems to have never deserted Phyllis through the next decades as the Dillons moved from Mexico back to Rye, to Colorado, to Canada, back to Mexico, to California, and finally, to Florida.

Lou Mandler

CHAPTER SIX

MEXICO: 1961–1966

The five years of living and working in Mexico gave all the Dillons happy memories. It gave them a better lifestyle, they formed lasting friendships, and it gave Dick valuable business experience.

As Dick said, "One of the wonderful things about Mexico was as an ex-pat, your income in Mexico City was small for America but large for Mexico. We had a nice house they paid for and a company car, things we couldn't get close to in Rye.

"I actually drove a truck and sold consommé packets off the back of a truck for the first six months. I had to learn the language. I had taken French at Canterbury. I learned Spanish on the street, and I went to a tutor. I became pretty fluent between having a tutor and being forced to use the language on my job."

Learning Spanish was different for Phyllis. "I hung out with my friend Chata del Rio all the time, and her friends spoke Spanish, so I learned kitchen Spanish. I never took lessons while I was in Mexico. I just sort of picked it up. Patty and Dickie became fluent in Spanish because they went off to school when they were 5 and 6, really little. They went to an English speaking Catholic school, but the school taught Spanish classes, and the children mixed with Spanish speaking children."

In addition to the amenities of having a house and car, Phyllis appreciated Mexico for the household help available there. After Scott was born in 1961, she had five children, ages six and under. "Going to Mexico really saved my sanity," she said, "because we had all this help. I had a cook, a housemaid, a lady that would come and do the laundry and the ironing and clean the silver. I had a bunch of help, and the cook and the housemaid lived with us. And we had fabulous houses."

Phyllis told one remarkable story about their first Mexico City house. "We found this house in the old section of Mexico City with a swimming pool. I said, 'I can't live in this house unless you fill in the swimming pool.

There's no way.' I had all these children, and the pool was right outside the living room doors. I was such a neophyte; I had no idea you couldn't ask for such things. But the people who owned the house filled in the swimming pool.

"Then, about 5:00 on the evening of the day we moved in, I opened the living room doors, and the whole swimming pool was covered with rats! There were five hundred rats all over out there. I could see them moving towards the wall of the kitchen garden, and if they got in there, they would get in the house. 'Dick! Dick!' I said. 'Get the gun, get something!' He went out there with a broom, but that obviously wasn't going to do anything. So he went to the drug store and got some poison and some bread. He loaded the bread with poison and threw the bread out there. How he knew to do that, and how he did it, I don't know. I was so hysterical I wasn't going to put my foot out there. The next morning there was not one rat, no dead rats, and I never saw them again. You cannot imagine how traumatic that was. They were just awful. I just know that the next morning, I thought it was a miracle that they were gone."

Dick surmises that because the pool had been empty for so long, the rats had made a home in the crevices at the bottom of the pool and when it was filled, they were forced to the surface.

After Dick's first assignment at General Foods in Mexico, selling consommé packets on the streets, he became advertising manager and, in 1963, marketing manager. He seems never to have been a compliant corporate "yes man." During his time as advertising manager, Jorge Kovacs left as head of Mexico General Foods, and he was replaced by an Englishman, Ted Arnold. He was "nice but stiff" said Dick. "The company had fallen on bad times, and we were in a cost cutting program. One time, he kept yelling about pencils and paper, so I wrote him a memo on the back of a grocery bag from the supermarket, and he came into my office mad as hell blazing, 'What are you doing?' Finally, he got my point, laughed, and walked away. Then, for three years, my boss was Mike Hazard, the general manager. He and I became very close after some real shoot-outs. I told him to go to hell at one point and stalked out of his office, but it never put my job in jeopardy. We remained friends.

"As marketing manager, I had a good deal of autonomy. Once I had to go up to White Plains to pitch a big deal promotion. I was to plan and present a program to send a lot of money to Mexico—millions of dollars—to break through the Nestle control of the coffee market. Our coffee product was called Café Oro (Gold). In the board room of General Foods International, the President of the International Division, Jim Delafield, sat surrounded by his minions. I made my presentation, and Jim went around the room asking everyone's opinion, and everyone went thumbs down. Jim said to me, 'What do you think?'

"I said, 'I don't think any of these people really understand the market and how difficult it is. Understand that if we don't do this, we aren't even going to be a player in the coffee business in Mexico.'

"He said, 'I agree with you. Let's go.' So I did, and we succeeded in breaking Nestle's hold on Mexico's coffee market."

Dick and Phyllis were not lonely during their time in Mexico. Their outgoing and welcoming natures created a wide social net. Soon after their arrival in Mexico, they met Jack McSounas, President of S.C. Johnson, and the Dick Clarks, who became close friends and part of their social core in Mexico. Membership at the Churubusco Country Club broadened the circle. As Phyllis said, "Most of our friends at first were ex-pats—Frank and Sally Plummer, Mary Lou and Jim Gwyn. Then, their Mexican friends became our friends, and vice versa. When you're abroad, your friends become family because your family is far away." Particularly close friends were Pepe and Chata del Rio. Pepe's father was a diplomat and Mexican Ambassador to Czechoslovakia, among other countries. They met many people through the del Rios. Phyllis and Chata had lunch together almost every day. Daughter Patty remembers the two driving around in a little red convertible.

During the last two years of the Dillons' time in Mexico, they left their first house in old Mexico City and leased another close by, where they decided to install a volleyball court. Phyllis remembers, "We belonged to the Churubusco Country Club, and I went over to the club and said, 'I have to use your roller,' and I attached it, a great big thing, to the back of my little Peugeot and dragged it; it must have been two miles. Then I got the construction workers next door and the maids to come out. We worked together to roll out the base of the court. It was a joint effort. We really wanted that volleyball court.

"Every single Sunday everybody, ex-pats and Mexicans, came to the Dillons with their children. John Smith from Canterbury and his wife Anna

Luz were part of those gatherings. We had hot dogs and beer and volleyball. We'd have ten or twelve people every Sunday. We gave really good parties. I still give really good parties."

The Dillon children lived in Mexico during significant formative years. Patty noted that after her kindergarten year in a co-ed Catholic school "run by very scary nuns," she and Richard went to a French Lycee where they spent a year in an immersion class and then were mainstreamed into a full French program. "I learned to multiply in French," Patty said. "By the time I was ten, I spoke fluent Spanish and French and English with a British accent."

The confluence of ex-pats in Mexico provided a rich cultural experience. Patty said, "I had a really wonderful best friend, who was British. I loved going to her house for afternoon tea. They would wheel in the tea cart, and we'd sit around the living room sipping tea and eating cookies with her mother and older sisters. I had a mad crush on her older brother. After tea, we'd go up to her room and turn on Beatles music."

In 1996, Dick was offered an opportunity within General Foods that promised a top-level management job. Both Mexico and Europe reported to a Finnish man, Mr. Pykala. He offered Dick the post as his assistant with the thought that Dick would eventually manage one of the small General Foods companies such as the one in Spain. Dick accepted this challenge, and the Dillons made plans to leave Mexico.

Two more Dillons, Scott (1961) and Bill (1965), were born in Mexico. When Dick and Phyllis left Mexico, their six children, who ranged in age from one to eleven, would again experience international living in future years. Phyllis commented, "I definitely think that having lived abroad is why the kids still live abroad. Stephen hasn't lived in the States for most of his married life; Billy has been in Europe all these years, and Patty is still very connected to friends from Canada and Mexico."

Phyllis summed up their five years in Mexico, "If life was a tapestry, the most beautiful part of my tapestry would be my time in Mexico. It was so fabulous. When the kids talk about growing up, Mexico was the happiest time. I left with regret to go back to New York the first time."

CHAPTER SEVEN

RETURN TO RYE AND THEN TO COLORADO: 1966–1970

Returning to Rye and the General Foods White Plains headquarters was returning to familiar territory. Nevertheless, Phyllis commented, "It was one of the most difficult transitions I've ever been through. Rye had all these little clubs. If you didn't do this, you had to do that, but when we got to Mexico, Boom! That was all gone. You could do anything; you could go out with the French, you could go out with the Germans. You were always involved with different kinds of people. When I came back to Rye, it was like being put back in jail almost.

"The way I got beyond that was I went to work. I went to Manhattanville and learned methods for teaching reading. I really wanted Patty to go to Sacred Heart School, and I couldn't afford it–Mother wouldn't pay for it—so I got a job teaching first grade at Sacred Heart. That was a happy, happy, wonderful experience. Really, really good. I absolutely loved it. I love children, loved teaching, and we had good kids in the school."

During these years, the last three of Dick's time with General Foods, the family rented a former doctor's house on the border of Harrison and Rye. The doctor had had an office in her home, so the Dillon children had little offices in which to do their homework. The transition back to New York must have been softened by continuing relationships with old friends such as Janice and Scott Pierce.

1966 was a significant year in the extended Dillon family as well. John Dillon, Dick's father, suffered a major depression that year, and Dick's brother Jack took over J. C. Dillon Printing which folded within a year. Jack then formed a printing brokerage firm. John Dillon sold the New York apartment, and he and Betty took up residence in the Spring Lake house.

For Dick, the work as assistant to the regional head of Europe very soon became frustrating. "I traveled to Europe in great style as a consultant. It was a lush job, but I thought it was a waste of time. I didn't have any control over what these people were doing; I was just advising them. I couldn't make decisions so I decided I wanted experience domestically, specifically with the Maxwell House division, where the project managers were considered to be the Green Berets of General Foods. So after six months of this, in November of 1966, I told Pykala I was going to resign. He didn't want me to resign and said, 'Do you have a job?'

"No," I said, 'but if I'm half as good as you guys tell me I am, I should be able to find a job in one of the domestic divisions."

"The Jell-O division of General Foods was interested and so was Birdseye, but I wanted Maxwell. I went to Tommy Thompson, the president of the Maxwell House division. His attitude towards me was, 'Yeah, we've heard of you. You think you're a hot shot, but your experience in Mexico isn't worth much.'

"I said, 'Give me a broom, and I'll sweep the floors, but don't cut my salary because I've got six kids.' He liked that attitude so he gave me a job. I started there in December of 1966. I had been a big shot in Mexico with a big office and a couple thousand people under me. Here I was put in an alcove with a Baker Scholar from Harvard running the calculator on deals. [The Baker Scholar designation is Harvard Business School's top academic honor, given to the top 5% of the MBA graduates.] He was a bright guy, but he was enthralled with his intelligence, and nobody wanted him around. I did that for three years, and in the process, I became the boss of the Baker scholar, and I fired him. I told him, 'Tim, nobody wants to see you. You have a terrible attitude. You are egotistical and nobody wants to work with you. Get out of here and get bounced around, and it will probably be good for you.' Years later, he came to me and said that was the best thing that ever happened to him. It was pretty nice of him.

"As the product manager for Yuban, I was in charge of the Yuban brand and did all the planning and execution of the brand. You work with the sales force and advertising people. While I was working there, I put together Sub Rosa, a marketing program for a freeze dried product that I developed that later became International Coffee. It was a cinnamon flavored coffee which was very popular in Mexico. Ken Roman, a top account person at Ogilvy and Mather, had his agency do a speculative ad campaign for it. Ken went on to become chairman of the agency, and he remains a close friend.

I asked Dick about his management style and philosophy. "When I manage people," he said, "I like to have people who plan. My procedure was that the people who worked for me would develop a list of projects and every Monday we would go over their list of projects. I was always looking for what I called the home run ball, the big idea. Once I approved that, I created dates to meet certain goals, and I let them go on their own. I liked to say, 'Have fun. Do your job and have fun.' I believed in giving people creative rein. There are people who would say I was a tough boss. I'd say no. But I did not suffer fools gladly.

"However, General Foods was not a wide-open business community. It was pretty disciplined, and the chance to really spread your wings was limited. That's why those of us who were entrepreneurs left General Foods. It was somewhat stifling.

"Every January I'd get a call from Paul Ray, a headhunter from Texas. He'd say, 'Dick, Colgate or Pepsi or another company wants to talk to you.'

"I'd say, 'Paul, I have a pretty good franchise here at General Foods, and I don't want to give it up for a $5,000 increase in salary.' I was making only about $17,000 at the time. I was in my early thirties, and I don't think I was viewed as a hot shot because I was a maverick. I said, 'When you get a real honest-to-goodness opportunity, high risk, high reward, give me a call.'

"In January of '69, he called me and told me about an opportunity in Boulder, Colorado, which was high risk, high reward, a big increase in salary, a company car, country club, and I said, 'I like this.' In February, I went out to meet Martin Hart, the president of Shurtenda, (Sure is tender) chicken fried steak. He was like Tom Sawyer, from Kansas, with the straw still coming out of his ears. You wanted to believe what this guy said, but he was a bloody liar. I tried to get as much detail about the company as I could; I looked at the financial picture, and they had doubled the size of the company from eight million to sixteen million in a year. They thought they could be a hundred million dollar company because all their sales at that point were institutional—hospitals, schools, jails—that were after the quick-fix lunch. By taking the product to retail, we could blow it through the roof."

The Shurtenda offer to be president of the company fit Dick's ambition to run a company. "In April of 1969, I resigned from General Foods. I was very flattered because the president of General Foods brought me into his office, sat me down, and said, 'We want you to stay, and I'll give you the biggest brand in General Foods to manage (which was Maxwell House Coffee).'

"I said, 'I can't. I am committed to these people, and I'm either going to get fired or I'm going to make a million dollars in a year.' I remember him saying, 'You're leaving here with guns booming and flags flying, and good luck.'

"Phyllis was thrilled to move out to Denver. We went out, and Phyllis picked out a nice house which was big enough for our family."

Phyllis's memories of Boulder are that the first moon landing occurred when they lived there and that they lived next door to a family with five girls and one boy, a contrast to the five boys and one girl of the Dillon family. The father of that family was an artist who taught at the University of Colorado in Boulder. He had created the dioramas in the Natural History Museum in Boulder. Phyllis said, "He was very involved with the Indians. I remember Indians arriving in his yard with trucks piled high with buffalo skins. Buffalo skins! I kept thinking we should have a buffalo skin. Dick said, 'No, we don't need a buffalo skin.' We never got a buffalo skin. This guy had a wonderful collection of Navajo rugs and jewelry. His wife Dorothy had the most gorgeous jewelry. She didn't know how to drive, so I taught her how to drive. She was an artist and a wonderful lady. I just loved her."

Patty Dillon Allman was twelve years old when the Dillons lived in Colorado. Although they lived there for only a year, she recalls that year as a "magical" one. Their house was on one side of sparsely settled Sunshine Canyon. The other side of the canyon was a greenbelt with no houses. In the evening the children could climb the mountain from their backyard and look over the twinkling lights of Boulder from the top of the mountain. The Dillons' au pair had taught Patty to play the guitar so sometimes guitar music turned these mountaintop excursions into song fests.

Colorado was also where the Dillon children became proficient skiers. Patty remembers being awakened every weekend morning at the crack of dawn to ski at a nearby ski resort. She said, "My dad would take the four oldest—Richard, me, Michael, and Stephen—to 'conquer the mountain.' My mom was on little kid duty for Scott and Billy. I can remember my dad getting us to overcome our fears and take on the challenge of learning to ski. By the end of the winter, we 'owned' the place. I thought of my dad when many years later, I taught my kids to 'conquer the mountain' and shared with them the joy of 'owning' the mountain."

Alarm bells started ringing very soon after Dick arrived at Shurtenda. Dick said, "I went to work, and the first thing that hit me over the head was that they were hemorrhaging money. They weren't anywhere near the sixteen million dollar volume they'd had the year before. It had not been obvious in the financial report, and they hadn't told me that.

"I took a trip around the country and discovered that they had taken it to retail, and they had gotten the big sales because the product had gotten into warehouse shelves, but then it didn't move out. So I said, 'You gave me a hell of a story which is untrue, but I have a contract so I'll go ahead and take a shot at trying to fix it.' I hired a couple guys from General Foods and another guy from Colgate, and got Grey Advertising in New York City to work with us without charge. They said they'd bet on our future. We put together a commercial with the New York Jets, who had just won the Super Bowl, eating this junk and loving it. 'You want your kids to have strong bones and you want them to look like this' was the message.

"Meanwhile, Martin Hart, the guy who had straw coming out of his ears, hired an older man, Howard Bloomquist, from a consulting firm to come in and look over my shoulder. I was furious but I had to tolerate it. They then told me to talk to stock analysts on Wall Street to convince them what a great company Shurtenda was. If I sold the analysts on that, it would have a positive effect on the parent company, Hardee's, earning forecast. I said it was a crap shoot and not a good idea. They said, 'You can't say this.' They felt I was demeaning the company.

"We never talked to an analyst.

"They had also decided, before I came, they needed a big factory to meet the anticipated demand, and they started the project before they had a blueprint. It was more expensive than they anticipated, and it threw us into the red financially. We had been rolling along pretty nicely at reduced administrative costs, breaking even or a bit better. Then, after a year, Martin Hart sold the company to Hardee Food systems, and the CEO of Hardee, Leonard Rawles, came to Denver with Martin in April of 1970 to see what we were doing.

"We had done three small test markets west of the Mississippi—media ads scaled down for local markets as part of the effort to find a formula for selling a product. At the meeting with Martin and Leonard, which Howard Bloomquist also attended, they said to roll out the test markets and go nationally with the ads. I said, 'No, I can't do that. The test markets were not successful.' They said they didn't care.

"I said, 'That would be totally irresponsible. I won't do it.'

"They said, 'You won't do it. OK.' And they walked out.

"Howard Bloomquist looked at me and said, 'You know what's going to happen to you?'

"I said, 'Yes, I'm going to get fired tomorrow.'

"He said, 'I'm damned proud of you. You're right. What do you want to do after you get fired?'

"I said, 'I want to do the same thing. Run a small company.'

"He said, 'I'll have a job for you in two weeks.'

"So guess what? I got fired. Shurtenda went on for a couple years. It remained an institutional company and never became retail. It eventually folded."

Phyllis commented that they were in Boulder barely long enough for her to unpack. "He got fired a lot. It was hard, but he always landed on his feet. Somehow I never worried. We knew how to be poor. We didn't have much money when we started. We didn't have much money ever until he sold the advertising firm. But we lived as well as we could."

To pursue his goal of running a small company, Dick interviewed with Squibb Corporation, a company that had consumer products such as Tetley Tea and Lifesavers, in addition to pharmaceutical. Squibb's head of human resources in New York City offered Dick the vice president of marketing at Squibb.

Dick refused. "I want to run a company; I don't want to be a vice president. We haggled, and I walked out.

"A week later, Squibb's HR called and said, 'You're the luckiest son-of-a-bitch on earth. The guy that runs Beechnut Lifesavers in Canada has just resigned. You want to run that?'

"I said, 'Yeah. That's terrific.'

So in August of 1970, the Dillon family left for Canada, where Dick would work at Beechnut headquarters in Hamilton, Ontario, about an hour's drive from Toronto.

CHAPTER EIGHT

INCIDENT IN DEL NORTE: JUNE 1970

Before the Dillons left Colorado to move to Canada, they decided to see some of the country of southern Colorado. The three oldest children were allowed to invite a friend so nine children, Phyllis, and Dick embarked on a road trip in a rented RV. One evening, the RV got stuck in a hole, and Dick drove it back and forth repeatedly to get it out. The next day, they drove up Wolf Creek Pass on Highway 160 near Del Norte, Colorado, a scenic highway through the Rio Grande National Forest. Wolf Creek Pass is at an elevation of 10,856 feet. After arriving at the top of the pass, Dick put the RV in low gear and started down, going about 15 miles an hour.

"It started to accelerate, and I hit the foot brake and nothing. I threw on the emergency brake, and it burned out. In front of me was a big earth mover, and I swerved to the left to go around, but coming at me was a car with a man and a woman towing a trailer so I swerved back to the right and went over the mountain. The RV—all plywood and aluminum--bounced down about 300 feet. If we had gone over the mountain a little further down, we would have gone over a 7,000 foot sheer drop. So we were lucky.

"The state police came, and we were on the mountain for a couple hours. They took everybody to the hospital in Del Norte, which is a pretty small town. I remember going into the room where the kids were. I had a pretty good cut, and I was bleeding, and there was something wrong with my hip, and it hurt like hell. I could hear Phyllis having hysterics. A nurse goes by, and I said, 'How's my wife?'

"She said, 'She has a pretty bad head injury.'

"I said, 'What are you going to do about it?'

"She said, 'We have one of the finest neurosurgeons in the United States.'

"I said, 'Oh, really.' So I called my brother and told him about this Doctor Barnett. I said to get Jim Daniels, a New York neurosurgeon and one of Jack's best friends, on the plane and get him out here.

"Jack called me back and said, 'The Del Norte doctor really is one of the top neurosurgeons in the United States.'

"They decided they didn't have to do surgery on Phyllis, and I had a big chunk of the ilium bone taken out. Most of the kids were OK, but Scott had a fairly bad head injury, although not life threatening. We were in the hospital for a couple weeks or more. I was going around with a cane."

When it came time for Phyllis to go to Canada to look for a house, she was still feeling the effects of the head injury she had suffered during the Del Norte accident. Her good friend Tricia Eigo declared Phyllis could not go alone, and she arranged to travel to Canada with Phyllis. "Talk about good friends," said Phyllis.

Dick suspected there was a defect with the RV which caused the brakes to fail, so he called a lawyer friend in Boulder and asked him to take an expert with him to examine the RV's Ford chassis. The friend went down to Del Norte with a highly regarded engineer from the University of Colorado, and they told Dick, "You have a case."

More than a year later, the case was ready for adjudication, so the entire Dillon family flew back to Boulder, hoping to win the case and be awarded damages.

"John, our lawyer, built the case on the braking system going out because the system which provides air for the brakes was improperly connected and came loose. The presentation the first day was terrible. I told Phyllis if our lawyer were a product manager, I'd fire him. So I got a hold of him and told him, 'Get some whiteboard that you can diagram what's going on. Describe that using visuals.' Which he did, so on the second day, I thought we had a chance. The third day, the Ford Motor Company came in and brought the piece of equipment and showed the jury that it was all in place; this couldn't have happened."

Dick was infuriated that his lawyer and his engineer had evidently presented a case built on non-existent evidence.

"So I told John, 'Go tell the judge we're out of here. We concede this case.'

"He said, 'Don't do that. Ford will sue you for a million.'

"I said, 'I don't give a damn. Go tell the judge.'

"He told the judge this, and the judge found favorably for Ford.

"The Ford rep came over to me and said, 'Thank you for your honesty. We know you weren't part of this scam, and I've been authorized to tell you we'll pay for your expenses to bring your family up here and fly them back.'

"I said, 'I appreciate that. Can you tell me what happened?'

"They brought over this elderly man, their expert who worked on this case for over a year, and he said, 'You testified that the night before the accident the back wheel had been in a hole, and you were rocking the vehicle between first and reverse. We think you burned out first, the low gear, and when you had to go into low gear, you were free-wheeling, and you didn't know the difference.'

"So that was the end of my friendship with that lawyer."

Lou Mandler

CHAPTER NINE

CANADA — BEECHNUT/SQUIBB: 1970–1972

When Phyllis and Tricia Eigo went house hunting in Toronto, they found a "great house" in the Rosedale area of the city on Schofield Place. It was near a park with tennis courts and an ice rink. "It was fabulous for the children. It was right on the subway line, and the children learned how to ride the buses and subways."

"The Canadians are so civilized," Phyllis went on. "It is the most civilized country you can possibly imagine. In Canada, our neighbors got the boys a membership in the Canadian Yacht Club, which we couldn't have afforded, so they could go to camp in the summer. That was the kind of thing people did. The children went to public schools and were very well accepted. Some of Patty's closest friends today are her Canadian friends. However, later, in the private schools they did encounter anti-Americanism.

We were there during interesting times. Quebec was threatening to leave Canada, and there was lots of anti-French feeling in the country as a whole. Overall, Rosedale was wonderful. Dick has never taken me to a place that was awful to deal with."

Patty Dillon Allman echoed Phyllis's positive perspective of their two years in Canada. "I loved it," she said. "It was fun being an American in Canada—everyone was curious about the United States so it made it easy to make friends. I met my best friend in Canada. In fact, I just returned from a week in Copenhagen with her. . . We met in 8th grade and remained very close through high school, college and everything else—despite living in the same city for only two years. So Canada had a lasting effect."

Phyllis and Dick had an uncanny knack for connecting with and becoming friends with well-known individuals who could be called movers and shakers of government and business. Neither Phyllis nor Dick makes an issue of this. Asking questions and, in some cases, researching a name they had mentioned often unearthed interesting individual profiles or stories. Such was the case with Ontario neighbors, Dalton and Linda Camp.

When they first met the Camps, neither Phyllis nor Dick had any idea that Dalton was a national political figure. However, soon after meeting them, Toronto's Sunday *Globe/Mail* arrived, and Dalton's photo was on the cover of the pictorial section of the paper. Phyllis called Linda and said, "Is this really your Dalton?" Dick's summation of Dalton is, "one of the smartest people I've ever known." Given the extent of Dick's acquaintances and friendships, that is quite an accolade.

Phyllis said that the Camps "adopted us."

Phyllis and Linda's friendship began when Phyllis was looking for someone to play tennis with, and another neighbor connected Phyllis with Linda Camp, the beginning of a very close friendship that continued after the Dillons left Canada. Dalton and Linda Camp had five children, and the Camp and Dillon children had much in common. When the Dillons went camping through Europe, Michael Camp, who was the same age as Richard, went along. Years later, Linda Camp attended Patty's wedding, and Linda and Phyllis maintained their close relationship.

When the Dillons knew Dalton Camp, he was already known for helping John Diefenbaker win elections in 1957 and 1958, and also, in the 1960s, for helping to remove Diefenbaker as leader of the Progressive Conservative party. Always politically active, Camp was a close friend of Prime Minister Brian Mulroney, and he wrote a twice-weekly political column which was syndicated across Canada. A book by journalist Geoffrey Stevens, *The Player. The Life and Times of Dalton Camp (2003),* chronicles the life of this brilliant and influential Canadian.

Dick enjoyed his position as president of Beechnut, where he supervised about a thousand people and earned the trust of George Perry, Director of Squibb Corporations. However, Dick said, "My immediate boss was kind of a narcissistic devil. I got into a couple shoot-outs with him in the New York office. Others on the floor would hear it and say, 'Dillon must be here.' George Perry would say at annual budget review, 'I know you're going to make your numbers. Just tell me where and how much you have hidden.' Which was fun. I created a product called Breath Savers which is on the market still today. I filled in the hole in Lifesavers with Breath Savers. I had a great time at Beechnut.

"I had a charge, in addition to new products, to come up with a company to buy to expand the business in Canada. I traveled around Canada and found a company in Montreal called Grissol Foods, and I took a plan for the purchase of Grissol to headquarters in New York. George Perry told me that Squibb's policy was that my board of directors' manager would do the presentation to the board. 'You don't,' he said. 'Sit down. Cool your heels, and I'll be out.'

"When he came out, he said, 'I've got good news and bad news.'

"I said, 'Give me the good news.'

"He said, 'They loved your presentation.'

"What's the bad news?"

"Your presentation is the straw that broke the camel's back. For two years the Board has been discussing the elimination or sale of all their food products and concentrating totally on pharmaceutical. This has brought that to a head."

"What are you going to do about me?" I asked.

"We thought about that," he said, "and we are going to keep one small food company in England that is doing very well. We'd like you to go over there and run it."

"I said, 'George, I don't want to run it. I don't want to be the food guy in a pharmaceutical company.'

"So he said, 'OK. Take some time to think about it.'

"We thought about making our life in Canada because we had a good life and wonderful friends. But the difference between Canadians and Mexicans is that in Mexico, they have no choice but to bring you into the tent. In Canada, they don't dislike you; they just don't want to bring you into the tent. They are nice people and all that, but I decided running a Canadian company would not be so comfortable. Plus, I decided the one guy who offered me a job was a crook. Later, though, I ran into some Canadians on a cruise who knew him well, and they said he was very successful. So maybe I was wrong.

"Serendipity is something else. About this time, I got a phone call from my friend Mike Hazard, who had been my boss at General Foods in Mexico. He had gone into the executive search business, and he said, 'I'd like you to come down and talk to the people at Johnson and Johnson--the president of Johnson and Johnson in Mexico.

"I said, 'I don't want to go back to Mexico.'

"The guy I had lined up pulled out at the eleventh hour," he said. "Do me a favor and come and talk about it. Be a warm body and go down and be nice to them."

"I sat with John Avery, the guy who was responsible for Mexico, and I said after about half an hour, 'John, I'm here under false pretenses. I have no intention of taking the job, but I would like to explore what is available in domestic.' Probably the quickest way to get a job is to tell them you don't want it. I started out at 9:00 in the morning, and at 9:30 I made my declaration, expecting to get an 11:00 flight back to Newark. I left there at 6 or 6:30 that night after saying I'd take the job as president of Johnson and Johnson in Mexico.

"So I went back to Mexico with Phyllis and the kids."

Patty Dillon Allman remembers that her father gave the children a choice of moving back to Westchester County or to Mexico City. She said they all voted for Mexico City. "Somehow, going back to Westchester seemed boring," she said. Whether the children actually clinched the decision or not, clearly they approved of Dick's acceptance of the Johnson and Johnson offer.

CHAPTER TEN

MEXICO, SECOND TIME AROUND: 1972–1976

On the move back to Mexico, Phyllis commented, "I was a little leery about returning to a place I had loved so much." Her apprehension was undoubtedly buttressed by the different situations of the children at that time. They were in various stages of schooling, and only Scott, Billy, and Patty lived full-time with Dick and Phyllis during this period. She said, "The children loved Canada. Richard loved his school in Canada, and he had only one year of high school left. Richard went through all four years of college at the University of Western Ontario. Stephen was in a boarding school in Canada, and Michael was on a ship abroad kind of thing. After Patty graduated from the American School in Mexico, she went back to Canada and went to Queens in Canada."

In the Dillons' second round in Mexico, they lived in the Coyocan area of southern Mexico City. Most Americans lived in the Las Lomas area, but Phyllis did not want to be surrounded by Americans. Instead, they rented an old Mexican colonial house designed by architect Manuel Parra. Phyllis described one of its memorable features: "You walked in, went upstairs, and there were these huge fresco paintings. One of them was of St. Sebastian who was knifed 800 times, and little Billy Dillon had nightmares about it for a while."

Their house in the Coyocan area was right next to the Churubusco Country Club, next door to a hospital, and in the same neighborhood as the movie studios. Phyllis said, "My kids would go over the walls—everything there is walled-in—and peek into the studios where they had all the scenery, and come back and tell me, 'You wouldn't believe what was in the studio.' Then they would look out the window at the hospital and tell me hair raising stories about what they saw—children being born and so forth. It was interesting."

That some of the children were teenagers during the turbulent '70s was an added concern for Phyllis about Mexico this time. "We were very worried about drugs. If you were caught in Mexico with marijuana, you were put in jail immediately and never, ever got out. In Mexico, you were guilty until proven innocent. You are told when you move to Mexico, if you have an accident, get out of there. I was really afraid. I knew Michael had started to smoke pot, so I was very concerned about the boys being there. So they stayed in school in Canada. I was ever vigilant when the boys were home. You have to be very, very careful in Mexico."

For daughter Patty, Mexico continued to be "a big and very beautiful part of my life tapestry, a magical place." In Mexico in the 70s, Patty went to the American School which was about 50/50 ex-pats and Mexican students. She continues to return for class reunions, and she spent six years in the early 2000s on the board of the American School in Mexico City. Patty remembers, "My closest girlfriends were Mexican. One was a photographer, and we once went into the main square at the center of the City—the Zocalo—where every one of the old cobble-stone streets is dedicated to a different product; there are stores for bananas, chilies, dresses for brides. At night, we'd sometimes go to Plaza Garibaldi—in the Zocalo where the Mariachis convene. You could give them ten pesos, and they'd sing for you. The old colonial parts of the city are so wonderful.

"I remember going to the house of another friend, who taught me the proper way to eat a mango. They have special mango forks with three prongs; the one in the middle is very long. You pierce the bottom of the mango with the long prong, peel it, and eat it like a popsicle. So delicious!"

This time around in Mexico, Phyllis and Dick continued to enjoy friendships with the ex-pats—people Dick had gone to school with, the Lathams, Mary Lou and Jim Gwyn, John and Anna Luz Smith, the Dick Clarks. Unfortunately, because of changes in their husbands' careers, good friend Chata del Rio "was barely in my life," said Phyllis.

The Churubusco Country Club again played a central role in Dick and Phyllis's social life. Phyllis and Dick jointly recounted a memorable incident. Phyllis began, "Our backyard abutted the caddy place on the club, and the caddies hung out right by our backyard. Dick played a regular game with a group of men the first time we were there. When we came back, they wanted him to join them again. But they played for big stakes, and we didn't have that kind of money, so Dick said he couldn't do that."

Dick picked up the story, "I played every Saturday with two Mexican friends, and some Americans asked me to play on Sundays. They played for $100. I asked, 'Who are the players?' They said the fifth player was a guy named Sam DePalma, who had come in '66, the year we left Mexico."

Another Churubusco member, film producer Robert Lerner, brother of lyricist and playwright Alan Jay Lerner, had given Dick some background on Sam DePalma. He told Dick that members of the club suspected something was fishy with DePalma because once when a group was playing poker at DePalma's house, he asked Lerner to get something out of a closet. Lerner opened the wrong door and saw bundles of bound hundred dollar bills.

Then, in 1969, *Life* did an article on the Mafia and ran a picture of Sam Giancana, the head of the Chicago Mafia. Sam "DePalma" was clearly Sam Giancana. Despite his notoriety, Giancana came across as a "nice guy." The Churubusco group accepted DePalma/Giancana, a golfer who shot in the low 80s, as part of the golfing group to which Dick was invited.

When Dick came home after his club friends had asked him to join them in their Sunday golf outings, his friend Dick Clark, an FBI agent, happened to call. Dick Dillon said to him, "Let me tell you a story," and proceeded to relate the invitation to play golf with Sam DePalma. Dick Clark immediately got excited and said, "Play for the big money. If you win, keep the money. If you lose, the government will reimburse you. I've been following this guy since he arrived in 1966. Play with him, listen to everything he says, and Sunday afternoons, I'll come over and debrief you."

"You're nuts," Dick told him. "I'm not interested in wearing concrete boots."

"A month or two after," Dick said, "two Mexicans knocked on Sam's door at 7:00 in the morning and told him they were interested in buying the property next door and wanted him to show them the demarcation line. When he left the house, they grabbed him, took him to Mexico City, and then to Chicago. He was earmarked to testify against the Chicago Mafia, but before he testified, he was killed with a bullet to the head."

Sam "DePalma" Giancana had a colorful history. He made headlines after the Kennedy presidency for several reasons. Judith Exner claimed to be the mistress of both Giancana and Kennedy. It was reputed that Giancana participated with the CIA in plots to assassinate Castro. He has achieved a kind of immortality by being the subject of several books, movies, and TV shows. The 1995 movie *Sugartime* depicts his relationship with singer Phyllis McGuire, who was introduced to Giancana by Frank Sinatra. Other movies he figures in include *The Rat Pack (1998)* and *Power and Beauty (2002)*. His daughter Antoinette wrote *Mafia Princess,* and Norman Mailer's book *Harlot's Ghost* depicts Giancana. Giancana served time in prison in 1945 and 1966, after which he went to Mexico. When he went to prison in 1966, he purportedly told his children he was "at college."

Dick relished his position as president of Mexico Johnson and Johnson. He had achieved his goal of attaining a position where he could make critical decisions and affect the course of a company. In describing his experience, he said, "Johnson and Johnson was an umbrella company with lots of products. Beside pharmaceuticals, they had a baby product line, oral diagnostic products [for example, for testing blood levels], and other consumer products. Even though my expertise was in food, I specialized in consumer products, and J and J's products did well. We had a great growth rate, retail grew, and we maintained the institutional market.

"I supervised two or three thousand people at Johnson and Johnson in Mexico. I ran a pretty good show. My method of operating was that I would bring people in and gain confidence in them, and if they performed, they were off and running on their own. I was lucky that I had good creative people. I was a micro-manager only in that I wanted them to come up with big ideas. My main contribution was coming up with advertising concepts for products like Tylenol and Stay Free. Stay Free Maxi-pads was a big one. This is where I did the test marketing that I was able to use later in the Mendoza Dillon advertising company. I tailored the test marketing practices from the States for Mexico."

Dick's yen for and talent in dramatics that had been recognized at Canterbury re-emerged at this time. Mexico City had a very active 500-seat theater with a professional director. The performances went on for two weeks. "I had good parts. I was the lead in 'The Last of the Red Hot Lovers'. My *piece de resistance* was 'Little Mary Sunshine.' I did this on and off for four years; I had to learn all these lines, and I would line the kids up in the back yard and give them parts. Billy was in one of my plays."

These musicals gave expression to Dick's love of singing while also somewhat assuaging Dick's resentment that Mr. Mack at Canterbury hadn't put him in Canterbury's choir until Dick's Sixth Form year. Mr. Mack's reluctance brings to mind Patrick Hemingway's comment, "If you were a good student, you were in Mr. Mack's choir." Perhaps it was Dick's lackluster student record, not his singing ability, that kept Dick out of the choir for three years.

Canterbury followed Dick to Mexico in other ways too. His old friend, Michael Duffy, the boy in the green suit he met his first day at Canterbury, stayed in touch and visited the Dillons in Mexico City, as he had when the Dillons lived in Rye. Dick spoke warmly as he remembered his classmate. "Michael was a character, very sharp tongue, funny, not a stereotypical clergyman. We had a lot of fun. I was very surprised when he went into the priesthood." Because of their close friendship, Dick was regularly apprised of developments in Mike's career in the Maryknoll Order. "Michael first went to Tanzania in 1969, and he decided in Year One that saving the people's health was more important than saving their souls, so he spent a year reading books on growing different crops and appealed to his friends for donations to buy a tractor. Then he went out into these little towns and said he would give material to improve the productivity of the farms. His project was enormously successful. He got a line of credit for a couple million dollars and hired a couple German agronomists, one was a cattle breeder and one was a hands-on grower."

During Mike's time in Tanzania, he became acquainted with Tanzania's president, Julius Nyerere. Nyerere was the first president of the new republic of Tanganyika in 1962, and when it united with Zanzibar in 1964 to form Tanzania, Nyerere continued as president of Tanzania. In the early 70s, when Michael Duffy knew him, Nyerere was using the military to force the population onto collective farms, and villages were often burned down.

Dick reported that Mike and Nyerere used to go drinking together. "One night," he said, "in 1974, after a five-hour political shoot-out, Michael told the president that the form of Communism he was using wouldn't work, that he was much too strict, and he had to loosen up. Mike said that Nyerere's idea of forcibly moving everyone into a central location would take away the farmers' land, their only possession. Michael said, 'If you don't stop, I'm going to write to all the opinion leaders in this country and tell them you're inadequate for this job.' The president said, 'Come with me,' and took him downstairs where there was a dungeon, a prison. He said, 'Michael, if you do that, I'll put you in there and throw the key away'."

Michael left Tanzania, went to neighboring Kenya, got out a typewriter, and wrote the letters. According to Dick, "Afterwards, the head of the Catholic Church in Africa called him and said, 'It has taken us centuries to build up relationships with these people that you're destroying in a matter of weeks'." Michael went back to the States and got his PhD in 1975. He never returned to Tanzania, but he did return to Kenya. In 1999, Michael and Julius Nyerere died on the same day. John Duffy, Mike's brother, said that at Mike's funeral, his friends jokingly wondered how St. Peter handled their simultaneous arrival at the pearly gates.

Meanwhile, several events occurred at Johnson and Johnson that presaged the Dillons' departure from Mexico. Each involved Dick Sellers, the CEO of Johnson and Johnson. One centered on a company in Dusseldorf, Germany, which J & J had bought. The Dusseldorf company created a machine that made digitally inserted tampons. They invited sixty of J & J's one hundred companies to Dusseldorf to be introduced to the new machine. After learning about it, each manager met with Sellers. When it was Dick's turn, he said, "Sellers said to me, 'You're going to take two or three machines.'

"I said, 'That's not a good idea. We just weaned Mexican women off newspapers and paper towels for their menstrual periods, and they would view digital tampons as masturbation. Maybe in five or ten years.'

"Sellers said, 'You're going to take these machines.'

"I said, 'OK, I'll take the machines and put them in the basement and mothball them.'

Dick's independence in this incident could not have gone over well with Sellers. Soon, another issue occurred that hinted they were on a collision course. In 1975, Senator Frank Church of Idaho, better known for his work concerning revelations on intelligence activities, also led a sub-committee that investigated the practice of U.S. corporations in the international scene. The most famous outcome of that investigation became known as the Lockheed Scandal in which it was revealed that Lockheed had made payoffs totaling billions of dollars from the 1950s to the 1970s to foreign governments to guarantee contracts for military aircraft. The Lockheed Scandal sent shock waves through all multinational U.S.

corporations as they scrutinized their own practices. Johnson and Johnson was no exception.

As Dick tells it: "We also had a line in our budget for payoffs for our bandage business. It had been there since the 1940s. I had been asked to pay for other products, but I wouldn't do it. Because of the Lockheed publicity, a J & J executive committee—all inside guys—met about this, and I had to meet with each one of these guys. My recall is that each one said, 'Dick, don't worry; you won't get hurt by this. This has been going on for a long time.' The last person I saw was Dick Sellers. He said, 'Well, Dick, I never agreed with these payments anyway. We are going to stop them, and we are going to recast our budgets without them.' I said, 'I agree with you. I've been told there will be no personal ramifications regarding what has happened in the past.' He said, 'I didn't say that.' He was a jerk. But I continued doing my job."

It wasn't long before Dick's honesty, bluntness, and refusal to go along with a bad decision created yet more conflict with Johnson and Johnson's top command. Dick recounted a final incident:

"My next step at Johnson and Johnson would be to run all of Latin America. In 1975, John Avery came to me and said, 'We want to promote you to run Latin America. We'll put Donald O'Connor in your job.' O'Connor had been made my marketing manager by management decree.

"I said, 'I will not turn the company over to Donald because he is a liar. I can't support that.' So they put him back to headquarters and put another guy in his place. It was a real brouhaha. What I didn't realize is that Donald had all kinds of threads—ropes really—to the top through his godfather. He was finally fired, but Avery went on vacation, and when he came back, Donald had been rehired by the CEO.

"The company decided they had to get over this hump and called me up to headquarters in New Brunswick. The atmosphere there was like a line-up—the light bulb hanging from the ceiling and all. When they questioned me, I said, 'I can't change my opinion of Don. He is bad news.' They didn't like that.

"These things were building, and finally, in February of 1976, two bosses, John Avery and Frank D'Angelo, met with me. They told me to go up to New Brunswick. I came home that night and said to Phyllis, 'I'm going to get fired.' When I got to headquarters in New Jersey, I was told, 'Sellers (the CEO) doesn't like you. You have to get a new job by January of next year. Meanwhile, go back to Mexico and run the business. You're doing a hell of a good job. We'll give you a nice payment to take care of you.' Sounds wacky but that is what happened."

Of this firing, Phyllis admitted, "That was really traumatic because we had to leave Mexico and come back to the States, and we didn't have a job to come back to. They did keep him on salary while he was looking." However, as she said earlier, she "always knew he would be OK. I'm not always right, but I was right about that." And she was.

Backyard party at the
Dillon Mexico house.
Guests include Pepe and
Chata del Rio, back row
right, and John and Anna
Luz Smith, front row left
and front row right.

Junior League Folly in Mexico. Dick and Phyllis on the far right.

Phyllis and Dick at a Mexico General Foods dinner. Ted Arnold in the center. 1963.

Phyllis in Mexico sharing her love of horses with her children. 1962.

President Dillon giving annual sales award.

Dick and Michael Duffy in Mexico about 1962.

Top: The Dillon family reunion in Vero Beach in 2000.

Middle: Patriarch Dick with third generation Dillons at the Dillon reunion. Includes offspring of Jack Dillon and Renee Dillon.

Left: Dick at his 75th birthday. 2008.

Dick celebrates retirement in Florida with a dolphin.

Dick and Phyllis with Derrick and Brian Dillon and Ryan Elizabeth Allman in Newport Beach.

Skiing in North Star, California with grandchildren Derrick and Brian Dillon and Ryan Elizabeth and John Allman.

1991 Princeton gathering of the Class of 1955. Bill Burks, Peter Danforth, George Hackl, Willis Mills, Frank Mountcastle. Dick in the background.

Golf in Scotland with Janet and Scott Pierce, Nancy and Hugh Beath.

Close pals from Rye, NY. Scott Pierce, Dick, John Blumenthal, Hugh Beath.

Dillon Clan at Canterbury Medal Dinner. 2011. Children Patty Allman, Michael and Richard Dillon and nieces and nephews

Dick and Canterbury Headmaster Tom Sheehy. Canterbury Medal Dinner.

Dick and Phyllis at the Canterbury Medal Dinner

CHAPTER ELEVEN

MENDOZA DILLON — NEWPORT BEACH, CALIFORNIA: 1976–1991

D ick began to look for a job in the States. "I was bridesmaid a couple times, but I had no meaningful stateside experience. Finally, a headhunter I knew pretty well told me I could contribute to his business and still have time to look around. That sounded like a good idea so we looked at areas around Los Angeles. Then, Ed Noble, the head of a Mexico advertising agency, said, 'Come work for me and open a branch of our office in the United States'."

"At first, I said, 'That's a wacky idea.' I had some exposure to specialty marketing—to Jewish markets—at Maxwell House. That was a small market.

"He said, 'Why don't you read this survey I've done and then tell me what you want to do.' I read Noble's survey, and there was a twenty million potential. The size of the Hispanic market in the U.S. was the same size as the Canadian population; it was a substantial market.

"Smells good," I said. "Let's talk about it. It smells pretty good." He paid me half of what I had been earning from J and J, but I still had some dough left over from the payoff.

"So we came up to the States, and I went into business with Noble's son and a woman from his office; there were three of us at Noble and Associates. He expected to take four or five years to make money. I was making money after a year. The Nobles turned out to be pains in the neck. I brought in 95% of the business. I used the test market approach in San Antonio, which has a 50% Hispanic population. I targeted a clearly defined area of the city where I could check the movement of products in Hispanic shops and pharmacies.

"Finally, I resigned from Noble and borrowed money and created Mendoza Dillon, a Hispanic advertising company. Nick Mendoza had been creative director of the international advertising agency Young and Rubicam in Mexico. After he lost J & J's business, Nick went back to Los Angeles and started an agency that was unsuccessful. I called him in 1978 and told him I was starting an advertising agency and that I was going to call it Mendoza Dillon, whether he joined me or not. I wasn't going to put the Irish name first in a Hispanic advertising company. He wanted 25% of the company, and I wanted to give him 5%. We compromised at about 20%. However, Nick had trouble growing with the agency. He was more interested in producing commercials than in the business end. After a little more than a year, we had a shoot-out on the plane coming back from New York, and I exercised the buy-out clause. He was an excellent film producer, and we gave him a lot of business after he left the company."

Phyllis said about moving to California, "If I had been able to choose, we would have gone to San Francisco, but the Mexican population was more in the southern part. We knew some people from Mexico in Newport Beach, and we ended up living in a rented house next door to John Wayne for a year. I don't remember seeing him, but the kids did."

In the first years that Dick owned Mendoza Dillon, Phyllis decided to make some money because several children were in college, and Dick didn't have the business going yet. "I worked for Coldwell Banker, and that was interesting. I was a really good P.R. lady but not a good closer. I was terrible at closing the deal—getting the contract done with the money in the bank. I could sell but not close; I couldn't get money out of people. I really wasn't a very good realtor because I didn't want any listings, and that is one of the things you are supposed to do. So I got fired from Coldwell Banker after about three years. I did make a little money."

In the early 80s, Dick and Phyllis realized that some of their children had learning disabilities. After consulting with Dr. Peter Mueller in Princeton and gaining some knowledge about learning disabilities, Phyllis decided to get a Master's degree. She said, "I knew that if I was going to have any credibility as an advisor on learning differences, I would need a degree."

Phyllis entered a two-year program at a Marymount Loyola branch in Newport Beach. Most of her work was done there, but she had to travel to Marymount in Los Angeles occasionally for tests and other things. At times, when she travelled to New York with Dick, she could take classes at Loyola in New York. She commented that "the New York teaching was much, much better. It was more demanding. The best part about the Los Angeles university was that it identified schools in the area that were working with these kids so I could visit the schools and make recommendations."

Phyllis earned a Master's degree in Guidance and Counseling in the mid-80s. "I did some consulting," she said, "but because of Dick's travel and eventual retirement, I couldn't do it full time and didn't pursue it as assiduously as I could have. I would have had to work full time in order to make full use of it."

As Mendoza Dillon grew, Dick recognized that entertaining clients well would benefit his business. However, he said that things had changed since he worked for his father's printing company in the 1950s: "When I founded Mendoza Dillon, there had been a sea change in the traditional advertising entertainment. In the 30s, 40s, and 50s, it was the big two-hour lunch with two or three martinis and then back to work. I don't know how the hell anyone went back to work and got anything done, but they apparently did. When I came along in the 70s, I decided that my *modus operandi* in entertainment would be not to take the client out to lunch but to take the client and his wife out to very nice dinners. This was obviously after work, when we could have a drink or two and wine with a nice dinner."

Some major clients--General Foods, Johnson and Johnson--were based on the East Coast, and Dick had to travel frequently to New York City to meet with them. It soon became clear that it would be beneficial to buy an apartment in New York for business reasons. They found an apartment on 66th and Central Park West and furnished it very simply. Then there was the question of where to take clients for dinner. At this, Dick launched into a story about a restaurant that became a favorite.

"There was new management at a very fine restaurant in New York on 55th Street called La Cote Basque that the Kennedys had used regularly, and it was quite well known among the celebrity crowd. Jean-Jacques Rachou had bought it, and he was a very, very good chef, and the reviews of the restaurant were excellent. I had called a client, Steve Price, vice president of General Foods, to see if he and his wife wanted to come into New York. This was in November. He said they'd love to do that. So I said, 'Fine. Let's meet at La Cote Basque at 6:30 on Friday night. I'm going to Gillette that morning and afternoon. I'll get off the shuttle from Boston and go right to the restaurant.' Gillette was a very tough client. They had beat me up pretty well that day.

"I walked into the restaurant, and I recognized the maître d', named Joseph, from another restaurant in New York. We had a great reunion, and he said, 'Mr. Dillon, your wife called. Mr. Price called and said he and his wife could not come in to dinner tonight. His briefcase was stolen in White Plains, and they had to find it. Your wife said to come back and she will get corned beef sandwiches sent in.'

"I said, 'Joseph, I'm exhausted, and I'm going to eat here. Would you mind calling Mrs. Dillon? I'm going to the bar to have a martini. Tell her I'm at the bar, and if she'd like to join me, I'd be delighted, but I'm staying here for dinner.' So I went to the bar. The bartender was a delightful man by the name of Charlie, and he made a great martini.

"Phyllis arrived, and we went into the dining room and sat at a banquette. We were looking at the menu, and this man came in, in complete chef's regalia including the high white hat, and he introduced himself with a French accent, 'My name is Jean-Jacques Rachou. I am the new owner.' We exchanged pleasantries, and he said, 'May I help you with the menu?'

"On instinct, I closed the menu, gave it to him, and said, 'Why don't you choose?'

"He said, 'Is there anything you can't eat?'

"I said, 'No. You go ahead and choose.' He had a big smile on his face, and he started to walk away as I took the wine list.

"He said, 'May I help you with the wine list?'

"I said, 'Sure.'

"He said, 'What do you like?'

"I said, 'I like the Pauillac and the Petrus.' He turned to those, and they were like $500 a bottle.

"I said, 'Jean-Jacques, this woman is not my mistress. She is not a business associate. She is my wife. So go back to the $50 bottle of wine.' He got absolutely hysterical laughing, and he went back to the $50.

"Then he said, 'Come with me.' So we got up from the table, and he took us back through the kitchen, which was spotless, and we went downstairs into the basement. This was a building that was probably built in 1900; it had ten foot high ceilings. He had converted the basement into a wine cellar, and we were crawling in and out of the bins looking at the wines, laughing and having a great time. We went back upstairs and started our dinner, which turned into about an eight-course dinner with the wine changing with each course.

"Halfway through, I said, 'Phyllis, this is going to be the most expensive dinner for two in the history of the New York restaurant industry.' It was marvelous. The bill came, and it said, 'Dinner for two, $100.' Well, this was a thousand dollar dinner for $100.

"He wasn't too dumb. I proceeded to take all my clients in the New York area to La Cote Basque for dinner. There were a lot of them from Johnson and Johnson and General Foods alone."

Phyllis loved participating in the entertainment aspect of Dick's business. She said, "The apartment was used mostly for entertainment, but we'd also get our friends to come in. It was really fun." She continued, "Of course, this meant that Phyllis had to have an extensive wardrobe, which Phyllis loved. I had my buyer at Saks, and I had great fun doing that."

On the West Coast, skiing was an important part of their lives and Dick's business. "I would invite clients to Utah, where we had a home. First, we had one in North Star near Lake Tahoe, California, and then in Alta, a wonderful little town in Utah."

At about this time, around 1980, Bill Simon, the boyhood friend from Spring Lake, came into Dick's life again. He had worked for Solomon Brothers in the bond division and "made a fortune." Later, Nixon appointed him Secretary of the Treasury. Dick said, "At the time, interest rates were up to 20%, and it looked like the country was going socialistic. I wanted to do an educational film on good government, and I wasn't sure who I would get to work with, but I'd write the script about good conservative government. In fact, I called John Wayne and spoke with his secretary, and it was sad because she said, 'He would love to do this, Dick, but he is dying.' That took care of that."

Dick soon read Bill Simon's conservative manifesto, *A Time for Truth* (1978) in which Simon urges an "awareness of the strong connection between economics and political freedom . . . to lose one is to lose the other."

Dick said, "I read it, and I said, 'My God, this is just what I want.' I wrote Bill a letter and said, 'This is what I want to do; use your book and you as a spokesperson. If you're interested—I'm going on a trip—I'll be back in the office on Monday at 8:00 Pacific Time.' I got in the office that morning, and the phone rang. I picked it up, and said, 'Yes.'

"Dickie! It's Billy! I want to do this." So we hang up, and I start writing scripts for the book and sending them to him for approval. But it never happened. Bill's wife Carol got cancer soon after that, and he had too much going on to participate.

"Bill became a financial advisor to me, and we started annual June gatherings playing golf and then having dinner in New York with our wives. We had a wonderful relationship. I called his office one day and he was way the hell out in nowhere. I said I'd call back when he got back the next week. His secretary said, 'No, no, we have standing orders that whenever you call we're to find him, and he'll call back. So stay there for another five minutes.' I couldn't believe this, but this is what happened. The next thing I knew the phone rang, 'Dickie, what's up? It's Billy.'

"We had a lovely house in Newport Beach, modest for California, but nothing is modest in California, price-wise. A house came on the market for a million dollars. Bill and I were out playing golf one day, and I said to him, 'Phyllis wants me to buy this house. What do you think?' We talked about it, and he decided no, 'You don't want to disrupt your portfolio, and this is a lot of money so don't buy it.' I got home that night, and about 10:00 the phone rang, 'Dickie! Buy the house!' So I bought the house, and it is probably one of the smartest things I've ever done. Its value appreciated substantially over the next four years."

In 1983, Dick went to Chicago for Peter Carney's daughter Sasha's wedding. While there, he "ran into a wonderful musician. Going back to New York on the airplane, I sat next to him. I told him I'd love to play the piano. He said, 'Call this guy, and he will teach you chording.' I learned how to play a base chord, melody, and I got fairly decent – got about fifteen songs, almost all of them were Sinatra or Cole Porter. I love to sing, so I'd sit down and play those songs and sing. I did that for about ten years and got tired of it. I wanted to be able to express myself, innovate, play by ear, and I talked to a number of musicians about it, and a couple tried to help me but nothing took, so I dropped the piano and continued to sing."

It was also during the early 1980s that Dick renewed his relationship with Canterbury School. Youngest son Bill was a student there, graduating in 1984, and Dick became a Canterbury trustee in 1982. The Board President at the time was John Duffy, brother of Dick's old friend Michael. About his time on the Board, which he left in 1986, Dick said, "I'm a bad board person.

When you build a business, you say, 'let's go do that,' and no one challenges you, and you go out and do it and get it done. When you're on a board, it's 'Let's run this up the flag pole.' Not enough action. I never liked being on a board." Nevertheless, in the early 1990s, he bonded with Headmaster Tom Sheehy, and he rejoined Canterbury's board for two more years and remained a friend of Tom and the School.

As much as Dick believes in hard work, he also believes in "the good life." Golf had always been a Dillon family pastime. John Dillon, Dick's father had several holes-in-one. Dick himself started playing golf at age nine and became serious about it when he was fifteen. He spoke more than once about the golfing prowess of his brother Jack, and golf had always played a role in Dick's social and business life.

In 1987, Dick and three friends started making yearly, ten-day trips to Ireland and Scotland to play the major golf courses. "We would play 36 holes a day walking with caddies. When we came back to the hotel at night, we'd be so exhausted, we would go straight to the dining room and sit down for dinner. I guess there was a pretty strong musk from guys who hadn't showered for 24 hours. You wouldn't want to sit next to them." Golf would play an even larger role in Dick's retirement.

Dick's relationship with Bill Simon produced an interesting brush with politics for Dick. At their annual June meetings to play golf, each would bring a guest. In 1987, Simon called Dick and said, "Don't bring anyone. I've got two people, one and Al Haig."

"I said, 'You don't mean General Haig, do you?'

"He said, 'Yes. Why?'

"I said, 'Bill, I've seen him on television. He's terrible. He's an arrogant guy.'

'Oh,' he said, 'He's good. You're going to love him. See you there.'

"I remember arriving at the table at the Morris Country Club, joining Billy and this other guy. Then Haig comes in and sits down. He is absolutely delightful. I said, 'Billy, this guy is a nice guy!'

"Haig looks at me and says, 'Why'd you think I would be anything else?'

"I said, 'I thought you'd ask me to kiss your ring and that you'd be absolutely overbearing.'

"Haig, at that time, was running for the Republican candidate for president against Bush and a couple other guys. He had asked what I did, and I told him I ran an advertising agency. So we went on, spent a delightful afternoon.

"The next day the phone rang in the New York apartment, and the guy introduced himself as General Haig's aide. He said, 'General Haig would like you to be one of the consultants on his presidential bid.'

"I said, 'Am I one of a hundred and it will cost me a couple hundred thousand?'

"He laughed and said, 'It won't cost you anything, and you're one of eight. You're the last one.'

"Before I accepted, I called Rumsfeld and said, 'Rummy, I got this offer from Haig. Do you think I should do it?' Rummy had also been a candidate but had dropped out, and I had helped him out in California.

"He said, 'Yes. Al's a good guy. You'll have a lot of fun.'

"So I became one of Al Haig's advisors and did an advertising campaign for him. Obviously, I didn't do too well."

By 1987, Mendoza Dillon had "grown like crazy." After just seven years in business, Mendoza Dillon was doing about $35 million in billings a year, producing more than seventy TV commercials. Prior connections from General Foods and Johnson and Johnson helped. Their clients included Kool Aid and Country Time Lemonade from General Foods, Tylenol and Stay Free Maxi Pads from Johnson and Johnson, Heinz Catsup, Levis, Ford Motor Company. "We quickly became the largest advertising agency of its type in the United States. Bob Holmen from Canterbury was influential in getting us the Miller brand."

In the winter of 1987, Dick learned from Bob Holmen that he had sold his company, Backer Spielvogel Holmen, to a British Company that paid twenty times earning. Historically, advertising companies had sold for four or at most, five times earning. Dick was intrigued, and Holmen told him to see a lawyer in New York who had helped put the deal together for Holmen.

When Dick told the lawyer he wanted twenty times earning if he sold, the lawyer said, "There's only one guy in the world who will pay you that kind of money—Martin Sorrell, the same guy who bought Holmen's company. He's in London, and if you agree, I'll call him and tell him what you're up to."

"I said to go ahead. Sorrell wanted to have dinner with me, so he flew to New York, and I had the vital statistics on a piece of foolscap. When we sat down to dinner, he said, 'Tell me about your business.' I pulled out the piece of paper and said, 'Here's what it's all about.'

"He said, 'Well, if this is true, I'll buy your business.'

"I said, 'OK. Have your people do due diligence.' He did this, and he still said he'd buy the business. The company had been doing very well. I was pulling a couple million dollars a year out of the business. We had almost one hundred employees by now. So when he made me an offer, I got cold feet and decided not to do it.

"Then, towards the end of 1987, I lost two big pieces of business for all the wrong reasons. Basically, because I wasn't Hispanic. One was Pacific Bell on the West Coast and the other was Warner Lambert in New Jersey. This told me how vulnerable we were so I said I was ready to sell. I called Bill Simon for advice, and he said, 'Sell it.' So, all things considered, I sold it. They kept me on for three years as CEO, and I retired in 1991."

Robert Howells, who had worked for Johnson and Johnson, joined Mendoza Dillon in 1981, became the company's president, and the company continued to do well.

"In June 1988, right after I sold the company, I had a funny conversation with Rumsfeld. He called, and we passed pleasantries, and he said, 'I'm holding a seminar in Taos, New Mexico, and I want you to come and be one of the members from the business community.'

"I said I'd love to, and he said, 'It'll cost you $5,000.'

"I said, 'You can take the $5,000, and you know what you can do with it.'

"Dick," he said, "I know you made a lot of money.'

"Yeah," I said, "but I'm not going to spend it that way.'

"The next day, the phone rang, and the guy introduced himself as the executive director of Rumsfeld's think tank in San Francisco, and he said, 'I understand you had an interesting conversation with Don yesterday. He really wants you to come to this.'

"My mind hasn't changed," I said.

"He said, 'Don has authorized me to tell you that in your case, he has waived the $5,000, and he and Joyce would like you to stay at their house.'

So I did it. I don't remember much about the seminar itself. I was one of about six people on the panel. It was sort of a bullshit expedition.

"We saw him later during the Iraq War. We had dinner with them in Washington. My daughter Patty was very reluctant to come because she is a liberal, and she didn't think she'd enjoy an evening with a conservative. We went into this restaurant, and he walks in and says 'Dillon!' and embraced me. Patty was very taken by him. I liked Rumsfeld."

CHAPTER TWELVE

RETIREMENT IN VERO BEACH, FLORIDA: 1991–2017

B y 1991, Dick had completed his term as CEO of Mendoza Dillon, and it was time to think of the next life stage for him and Phyllis. "We were living in Newport Beach, California, and we segued into retirement. I told Phyllis I didn't want to stay in Newport Beach. She said, 'Why not? The tennis court is down the street, the golf course is five minutes away, and we have a beautiful home right on the beach.'

"I asked her how many people from Newport Beach she would want to take on a week's vacation. She said, 'No one." And I said, 'That's the problem--the culture. I have just one really close friend here—Toby Walker.' I knew there were great beaches in Florida on the Atlantic Ocean. I had a dream of having a big house on the beach where all our kids could come and have holidays with us. Phyllis was really taken aback."

Phyllis remembers thinking, when Dick mentioned Florida, "That's where people go to die." But they took a trip to Florida to check it out. They stayed with Bob and Barbara Holmen in Vero Beach, and from there went down to Jupiter Island. A Princeton friend had recommended the real estate agent who took them around. Phyllis was adamant about not living in a gated community. "I am not a Stepford Wife kind of person," she said. The agent took them to houses which would have tables set for formal dinners, and at one place, Phyllis commented, "We could make this place into a strip mall." The agent finally said, "I think you two would be happy in the old Riomar section of Vero Beach." Dick called Bob Holmen that afternoon for a recommendation for a real estate person in Vero Beach.

Dick said, "We met the agent in Vero Beach about 9 in the morning. As we drove around the area, I could see Phyllis was pleased. There was a school, a church, a country club, a community. The agent took us to this one place, a great piece of property, right on the beach, but the house looked like a tear down. Phyllis went through the house while I sat in the living room and played the piano. When we walked out to the car, the agent said, 'What do you think?'

"I said, 'What is the property worth?' She said $900,000, and I said, 'Would you be embarrassed to take him an offer for the value of the property?' She did, and we compromised for a million. A pretty good buy. We got the finest architect in the area, and he did several plans, but we didn't like any of them. They were all too frou-frou. Finally, I said, 'Let's live in the place for a year, and then we'll decide what to do.' We ended up putting together a plan that we liked, and we didn't have to use an architect except for the structural aspect. We did a renovation and lived in the house on the beach for twenty-six years. It couldn't have been better. It was fabulous."

Phyllis agreed about the move to Florida, "Once again, the guy was right. I had to eat crow. I absolutely love it. We have the best of all worlds. The worst thing was, I got here, and the ocean was in the wrong place—I was always going in the wrong direction. The Pacific Ocean was west--over there, and here the ocean is east! It was very disorienting for awhile."

"I didn't want to risk my capital by going back into another venture," Dick said. "We had great friends, a great house, an apartment in New York City. We traveled. We had a hell of a lifestyle. We went to England, France, Italy. Our son Billy was in Florence. Stephen had a restaurant in France and then in Aberdeen, Scotland."

Dick and Phyllis's friendship with Scott and Janice Pierce resulted in a memorable vacation during George W. Bush's Presidency. When Barbara Bush, Scott's sister, learned the Pierces and the Dillons were planning a trip to Hungary, she had George Bush arrange for the two couples to meet with the American Ambassador to Hungary in Budapest. The Ambassador then entertained them with dinner. The following day in Prague, the American couples were again honored guests at a formal dinner. After dinner, they were introduced to an American couple who were working for a turbine company in Hungary. That couple, in turn, introduced them to a couple from Boston who were part of the Czech royalty and had come to Hungary to reclaim familial property. As a result, they owned a castle-like home. A house on their property had been home to composer Antonin Dvorak. Dick recalled with a chuckle that the bratwurst cooked in beer they had in Clock Tower Square was "the best I've ever had."

Golf was an important part of life in retirement. Dick won the golf championship at the Riomar Country Club in 1995. "I stood there, on the nineteenth hole, and the tears just flowed," he said. "Then I won it again on the 18th hole in 2002, both times against four handicap golfers."

In 1993, Dick once again became connected with Canterbury School. "When Sheehy came along as Head of Canterbury, he and I became good friends," Dick said. "So I gave and worked and became a strong supporter of the School." A memorable annual event illustrating his support of the School was the March reception for Canterbury alumni that Dick and Phyllis hosted at their Vero Beach home for more than twenty years.

On January 26, 2011, at a dinner at the Union League Club in New York City, Canterbury awarded Dick the Canterbury Medal, which "recognizes an individual, group, family, or class in recognition of outstanding service to the School." His Medal plaque on the wall of Canterbury's Steele Hall bears these words from Tom Sheehy, "Dick warms every room, every event, every meeting, chance or scheduled, with his zest for life, varied interests, sense of humor, and authentic concern for others. . . Dick is a Cantuarian for all seasons." Dick gave the commencement address at Canterbury's graduation in 2014.

In the early 90s, Dick and Phyllis's children were grown, but they became *de facto* guardians of two grandchildren—Derrick and Brian Dillon. Dick and Phyllis sent Derrick, the older of the two boys, first to Canterbury and then to two other New England boarding schools. After high school, Derrick "bounced around for about two years." Then, Dick said, "He was a ski bum in Colorado, and he came back to visit with us, and he was a bad boy, so I sat him down and said, 'This is not working; you have to get structure in your life. You should go into one of the armed services.' So he decided to go into the army, and it changed his life for the better. He served both in Iraq and Afghanistan."

Dick has saved an email Derrick wrote to him in 2008 while Derrick was in Iraq. It illustrates both the "life change" and the effect Dick had on his grandson. It reads in part, "I was actually thinking about you the other day when I was out in the middle of Iraq somewhere. . . . I started to think of all the people that I really cared about, and how they have been not only inspiration but a guide to where I am today. The one person that has really had a huge impact on me is you, Ha (his nickname for Dick). . . . I haven't always told you that I am extremely grateful for sending me to the schools you did and the effort you put into my and Brian's life. . . you were always patient and understanding without lacking the strictness to kick me in the right direction. . . I remember one time at your house I saw an article in your office that was written about you and your career. At the time I was amazed at what you had accomplished. . So I copied it and put it in my wallet. Now as I look back, that astonishment has turned to inspiration."

Dick and Phyllis also sent younger brother Brian to Canterbury where he excelled in art but finally chose to return to Florida to live with his grandparents. He, too, went to more than one high school before graduating. After living with Dick and Phyllis for four years, he lived with his aunt Patty and her family for a year or so before attending and graduating from the University of Maryland's art school in Baltimore. Phyllis speaks with great pride and some relief about how well both grandsons are doing today. Both have successful careers and happy marriages.

Dick's influence was not limited to that on Derrick and Brian. Patty Allman commented that she is grateful that her children learned from her dad how important it is to have the courage of one's convictions. She stated that her dad stuck by his beliefs whether it meant being fired or jeopardizing a friendship or being accused of being politically incorrect. It was a rite of passage, she said, for her children to "take on my dad at the dining room table and argue their point of view against a formidable opponent. They still don't agree, but there is great love and mutual respect. He taught us how important it is to have strong convictions and to live by them."

By 2000, Dick was the unofficial patriarch of the extended Dillon clan. John Dillon died in 1976, brother Jack died in 1996, and sister Renee in 1998. Jack and Renee each had seven children. With Dick and Phyllis's six children, that generation consisted of twenty. In 2000, Dick and Phyllis hosted a Dillon reunion at their Vero Beach ocean-front home. About 82 family members came from Atlanta, San Diego, Block Island, New Jersey, Europe, all over. In 2017, Dick and Phyllis have eight grandchildren. Patricia and Bill Allman have Ryan Elisabeth and John Pat; Michael has Isabella; Stephen and Pascaline have Gaëtan and Brendan, Scott has Derrick and Brian, and Bill has Mia. Derrick has given Dick and Phyllis a great grandchild.

In the late '90s, Dick and Phyllis further enriched their retirement experience by acquiring a second home. After visiting Sasha Carney Woods and her husband in the area near Steamboat Springs, Colorado, they fell in love with the area. They bought land in Steamboat in 1996, and in 1998, they moved into the house they had built on the land. Subsequently, Phyllis and Dick established a routine of living in Colorado from June through October and returning to Florida around November 1. The Colorado place would bring them out of Florida's summer heat.

The Steamboat Springs place also enabled Phyllis to indulge her love of horses. She said, "Wherever we were, I usually managed to figure out a way to keep riding in my life. When we were in Canada, Linda Camp's daughter had a horse. She was away at school, and she wanted her horse exercised, and Ta, Da! I was able to ride her horse. I had Patty out riding with me then, and I even got Dick to come out, but that didn't last long. When we finally built the house in Colorado, that's when I really decided to get a horse."

Phyllis discovered a British woman, Joey K, who owned two Tennessee Walkers. "She came over to my house in Dakota Ridge, which has its rules and regulations. You're not supposed to have horses there, but Joey comes into my driveway with her two horses. That was the beginning, and I rode with her once or twice a week. Then she moved! She went to the Front Range and took the horses. The following winter she found Trigger for me through a mutual friend. Joey said about Trigger, 'Phyllis, this is the horse for you. Your name is on its rear end.' And Trigger was a fabulous horse, a Tennessee walker, a little Palomino. He was related to Roy Rogers' Trigger. He had papers."

Trigger was an important part of Phyllis's life for at least ten years. For about seven of those years, Trigger was brought to Florida for the winter. However, one year, Trigger got sick on the trip across country, and he was near death on arrival. Phyllis was distraught; at the same time, Dick had heart issues, and he had to go to Austin, Texas, for a procedure. Phyllis's attachment to Trigger and her priorities must have worried her children because Patty called her and said, "Mom, you have to go with Dad. You cannot stay with Trigger." Both Trigger and Dick recovered, but that was Trigger's last cross country trip.

In 2015, Dick and Phyllis took their family to Alaska to celebrate their 60th wedding anniversary. While they were gone, Phyllis had a call from Trigger's caretaker. At twenty-six years old, Trigger's life had ended. Phyllis said that when Trigger died, "I was so grief stricken that Dick had to be very nice to me even if he never was a horse lover. So now Trigger is up there with all my other little dogs and friends, and he'll be there if I ever make it."

For a time after they retired, Dick and Phyllis spent part of the spring and fall in the New York apartment, but eventually, they used it less, and the fees had increased from $120 a month at the time they bought it to $1,200. They sold the New York apartment in 2013.

At age 72, in 2005, Dick decided to learn to fly. "I went up in a Cessna and flew all over the place. Taking off is nothing. Flying around and doing exercises is nothing. Landing is everything. I couldn't handle all that was involved, and nobody cleared me for soloing, which was probably a good idea. I had about seventy hours when I quit."

A youthful passion that has continued into retirement is a love for baseball. Daughter Patty, who lives near Washington, D.C., began getting tickets for the Washington Nationals, and Dick has become a Nationals fan. "I had been a Brooklyn Dodgers fan and then the Los Angeles Dodgers, but after they were sold to this couple from Boston, I had enough of that, and the Nationals are an interesting team, so I shifted my loyalty to them. I have a dear friend, Christopher "Kit" Bond, who was the Governor of Missouri for eight years and then Senator for twenty-four years. He and I go to spring training games which is a kick because when we see the Cardinals play, we get special VIP passes and go out on the field and talk to the managers, and I feel like a big shot, I tell you. Phyllis goes nuts because when the season begins, I'll watch the Nationals every day."

Dick no longer plays golf. He said, "As you get older you get weaker—I don't care what you do—and that weakness on the golf course is pretty humbling. I moved on to bridge, and my golf game became a thing of the past. Now I play bridge four days a week. Bridge has these master points, and there is no halfway. I had to learn the conventions—not all of them, but enough that now I'm pretty good. I play pretty well, and I enjoy it."

As Dick had hoped, their Florida homes have been a gathering place for their children and their families, especially at holiday time. After living in their ocean-front Vero Beach home for twenty-six years, they sold it in 2016 and bought a smaller home nearby. For Thanksgiving in 2016, Bill came from Europe with daughter Mia, Patty and her husband and two children came from Baltimore, Michael was there from Syracuse, Richard from Georgia, Stephen, and Scott, Derrick and Brian's father, were there.

It seemed natural as Dick's story came to its last chapter to ask him about his legacy. When I asked Phyllis the same question earlier, she focused on the Dillon children. And she went on to say, "Those six children are what drove Dick to do as well as he did." When I quoted Phyllis to Dick, he laughed. And then agreed. He said, "We have a lovely family. Our children have good values, and I think that comes from a combination of Phyllis and me. And it is a thrill to see the nice development of the grandchildren."

When I pressed Dick to explain what motivated his successful career, he was thoughtful for a moment and then gave a well-articulated, compact response: "First, I had been raised in a nice environment, and I wanted Phyllis and the children to have the same things I had been given. Second, I had a desire to show my father that I could be successful."

But motivation alone doesn't guarantee success. "Why were you successful?" I asked Dick. "Well," he said, "I wasn't always the smartest guy in the room, but I would say persistence counted for a lot. Then, I think I have a creative streak. I like to accomplish things and think of new and better ways to do things."

I nodded my head vigorously at his response, but later, I thought a missing, unmentioned ingredient is that expansive, charismatic Irish personality. It is impossible to discount the effect of those unusually expressive blue eyes and the embracing—albeit sometimes 'you're a pain in the ass'—attitude. Then there is that quality which Dick describes as being a rebel but which others define as being a man of character who lives by his convictions. This is an Irishman worthy of his heritage.

Richard Emmett Dillon left this world on August 16, 2017 from his Vero Beach home after holding, in his words, "living wakes" for several days with friends and family.

Dick and Phyllis, JP and Lou Mandler at the Patrick Sheehy wedding in Jackson Hole, WY, where this project began. October 2016.

CPSIA information can be obtained
at www.ICGtesting.com
Printed in the USA
BVOW05s2142141217
502846BV00023B/371/P

9 781634 985468